JANUARY

FEBRUARY

MARCH

BRAZILIAN RED CLOAK
Megaskepasma erythrochlamys

YESTERDAY - TODAY - AND - TOMORROW
Brunfelsia grandiflora

 Sulphur butterflies are attracted to Cassia

DESERT CASSIA
Senna polyphylla

A Garden Diary

A Guide to Gardening in South Florida

featuring:

Easy-to-follow seasonal guidelines to keep your garden looking great, monthly tips, calendars for your personal garden notes and answers to the most frequently asked gardening questions

Special Thanks to:
The Sun-Sentinel
for allowing us to re-print the many questions
that have appeared in Bob's column over the years and to
Joan Brookwell, Starr Fisher, and Pamela DePalma
for their many contributions to this publication.

Copyright 1999 M.E. DePalma and Robert G. Haehle.
All rights reserved.
This book, or parts thereof, may not be reproduced in
any form without permission of the publisher.

Published by DePalma Enterprises
Wilton Manors, Florida 33305-2413
Printed by Spangler Printers, Kansas City, KS

Library of Congress Catalog Card Number: 99-96253

ISBN 0-9676022-0-3

90000 >

9 780967 602202

Photography:
M.E. DePalma
Joan Brookwell
Rose Bechard-Butman
Starr Fisher
Winn Soldani
John Doyle
James Gable

Cover: *"Jo Williams"* Hibiscus named after
Jo Williams, Florida Federation of Garden Clubs President, 1997-
1999; National Council of State Garden Clubs, Inc. Chairman.
Habitat for Humanity Landscape Project 1999-2001

JANUARY

- We still can enjoy some months of color if **annuals** are installed as soon as possible. Try ageratum, calendula, begonia, petunia, candytuft, alyssum, dianthus, celosia, salvia, vinca, marigold, nasturtiums, cosmos, gloriosa daisy portulaca and impatiens now. **Vegetable choices** are also abundant, including radish, tomato, onions, beets, cabbage, broccoli, peas, potato, turnips, lettuce, celery, mustard, cauliflower, Chinese cabbage, beans, squash, spinach, corn, collards, parsley, eggplant, pepper, cucumber and kohlrabi. Many **bulbs** can also be planted, such as tuberose, dahlia, eucharis, canna, caladium, gloriosa, agapanthus, zephyranthes, calla, crinum, allium, ginger, montbretia, watsonia, lily and daylily. You can plant most **woody shrubs and trees** if there is a good water supply handy. The reliable rains will not be back until June.

- Irrigate all new plants daily for the first two weeks after installation and then about twice a week if there is no rain. Water deeply when you irrigate and in the morning only to avoid fungal problems.

- January is a relatively quiet time for most insects. Thrips and spider mites are active on avocado, crotons, mango, copperleaf and other large-leaf plants. Blast water under the leaves or use a soap spray on them. Do not plant under the eaves where these insects can really proliferate with no rain to wash them off. Annuals can be chewed off at ground level by cutworms. Fungal root rot can attack impatiens, begonia and vinca in wet areas.

- Eliminate the usual dead wood, crossing branches and stems from plants such as bougainvillea and silverthorn. Remove all suckers and water sprouts from fruit and shade trees. Prune roses back by no more than one-third.

Green Thoughts: It is always interesting that so many plants we think of as weeds have been given more respect by the English. For example, native plants such as goldenrod and beebalm were collected by early English horticulturists and sent back to the motherland to be bred and hybridized. Now we are getting improved versions of our American weeds and paying premium prices for them. Funny how an old weed suddenly jumps in social stature after obtaining British cachet.

PLANT OF THE MONTH *See color photo on divider* Yesterday-Today-andTomorrow *(Brunfelsia grandiflora)*

Although this large shrub is a bit demanding, all your efforts will be rewarded when it blooms from November to May. The flowers open as purple, change to pale blue the second day and are white on the third day. Blooms can literally cover the branches when conditions are ideal. During this blooming season, the foliage will thin out.

Native to Bolivia to Venezuela, this is best suited to morning sun and some afternoon shade away from concrete. It likes a somewhat moist location and will wilt quickly in a dry spot. Expect a height of 8-10 feet if left unpruned.

- Origin — Brazil
- Foliage — A simple green leaf shaped like a lance
- Nutritional requirements — Happiest in acid soil, it appreciates an acid fertilizer suitable for ixoras and gardenias in March, June and October.
- Salt tolerance — Medium

- Drought tolerance — Medium
- Light requirement — High
- Growth rate — Medium
- Propagation — By seed or cuttings
- Major problem — None
- Environmental problems — None

GARDEN NOTES

JANUARY GARDEN NOTES

Tickle it with a hoe and it will laugh into a harvest...English Proverb

JANUARY GARDEN NOTES
He who plants a garden plants happiness...Chinese Proverb

FEBRUARY

You can **plant vegetables** such as peppers, tomatoes, parsley, spinach, corn, collards, beans, eggplant, cucumber, squash, endive, kohlrabi, turnips, radishes, lettuce, celery, beets, broccoli, onions, potatoes, peas, cauliflower, mustard, Chinese cabbage and cabbage. **Annuals** such as marigold, salvia, vinca, impatiens, nasturtiums, cosmos, celosia, gloriosa daisy, portulaca, ageratum, begonia, dianthus, petunia, alyssum, candytuft and hollyhock can also be planted. **Woody plants can be set out now** if there is an adequate water supply. Most **bulbs can be put out now** such as canna, agapanthus, tuberose, caladium, eucharis, calla, daylily, amaryllis, allium, lily, rain lily, montbretia, watsonia, crinum and ginger.

Scale and mealybugs are active now. Check sago palms, hibiscus, ixora, gardenia, copperleaf and chenille plant for activity. Tomatoes have hornworms and various fungal/wilt problems. **Keep the foliage dry and water in the morning only**. Wet weather aggravates these conditions. Spider mites continue to be busy, particularly if plants are located under eaves. Hose off leaves to blast the pests off.

If a freeze is expected, water plants thoroughly the day before. Pull mulch back from plants so warmth from the soil will radiate up to the plants. Leave dead leaves and branches in place to protect the plants from future possible cold snaps. Remove dead leaves and branches in mid-March when cold weather is past.

This is a good time for landscape renovation, weeding as well as general cleanup and removal or restraining of aggressive plants. Beware of running heliconias, costus and bamboo, which can spread rapidly. The clereodendroms are also rapid spreaders, but are pretty if restrained. Snowbush is another sneaky customer that drops suckers all over the place. Be leery of the big vines such as sky vine, air potato, moon vine, wood rose etc. that can cover telephone poles and climb through dog doors.

Green Thoughts: It's disturbing to see perfectly good plants returned to nurseries and garden shops because people think they are "dead." I was at a local nursery recently and saw a perfectly healthy azalea returned because it was finished blooming and new leaves were emerging. The purchaser insisted that the plant was no good and wanted her money back. This brings to mind someone who buys a dress, wears it to a party and returns it the next day claiming it's the wrong size. This behavior is just not kosher, folks, and it means we all pay more for plants in the long run.

PLANT OF THE MONTH *See color photo on divider*
Brazilian Red Cloak *(Megaskepasma erythrochlamys)*

This plant has an unfortunate name – Brazilian Red Cloak — hardly helpful for its marketing. The scientific name is even worse — *Megaskepasma erythrochlamys*. Despite the unappealing names, this is an attractive shrub. Its large glossy oval pointed leaves are topped by red spires of bloom from late fall through early summer. It can bloom all year with good fertilization. But be careful where you plant it. Its big leaves wilt easily and are pale green in full sun. The same plant in moist shade is spectacular. The only disadvantage is the size of this big grower — 15 feet tall and 10 feet across is not impossible. The density of the shrub quickly eliminates objectionable views. Plant 6-8 feet apart for fast results.

- Origin — Brazil to Venezuela
- Foliage — Large shiny, ribbed, oval pointed leaves
- Nutritional requirements — It's not fussy about fertilizer as long as it has shade and moisture.
- Salt tolerance — Poor

9

- Drought tolerance — Poor to medium after establishment
- Light requirement — Low to medium
- Growth rate — Fast
- Propagation — Seed, cuttings, seedlings
- Major problems — Mealybugs and scale, which are rare on healthy plants
- Environmental problems — None

GARDEN NOTES

FEBRUARY GARDEN NOTES
"All my hurts my garden spade can heal."
Ralph Waldo Emerson

FEBRUARY GARDEN NOTES

I can enjoy flowers quite happily without translating them into Latin."
Cornelia Otis Skinner

MARCH

Annuals to plant this month include: zinnia, marigold, coleus, cosmos, portulaca, amaranthus, gloriosa daisy, salvia, vinca, begonia, aster, ageratum, torenia, balsam. **Vegetables** include: tomato, watermelon, radish, lima bean, cantaloupe, snapbean, okra, sweet potato, summer squash, southern pea, mustard, onion sets. Most **trees, shrubs, palms and citrus** can be planted now, particularly if the rains continue.

- **Fertilize** all trees, shrubs, palms, citrus, groundcovers and other plantings with a high-quality all-purpose fertilizer such as Lesco 12-2-14. Fertilize lawns with a 16-4-8 fertilizer with minor elements. Follow application directions exactly.

- **Bug populations** are starting to increase again now that the weather is warming up and new growth is emerging. Grasshoppers will hatch and should be killed as soon as you see them. Aphids will attach to new growth. Mites are common on citrus, crotons, avocados, copperleaf and mango. Scale and thrips also appear now. Chinchbugs will soon show up in lawns.

- **Cut back** ornamental grasses to eliminate old leaves and stimulate new growth.

- **Mulch** flower beds to suppress weeds. Keep mulch 1-2 inches away from leaves and stems so the bark can breathe. Let a professional apply weed and feed products to the lawn if needed. Homeowners traditionally over-apply and can cause thousands of dollars worth of damage, killing lawn, trees and shrubs. Setting the mower permanently at its highest setting and reducing watering will go a long way to reducing the need for expensive chemical treatments.

Green Thoughts: The next time we have a full moon, go outside and check your plants. Scientists may disagree, but my casual observations indicate that some fragrant plants bloom during the week of the full moon. Check your angel's trumpets, night blooming jessamine, lady of the night, orange jessamine, and other fragrant bloomers.

PLANT OF THE MONTH *See color photo on divider* Desert Cassia (*Senna polyphyllla*)

This small tree has tiny compound leaves that provide a delicate tracery over the dark barked branches. Bright yellow blooms can occur all year but are most prevalent between mid-October and May. Blooms are bright yellow and quite large considering the delicate foliage. Desert Cassia likes dry conditions, as its name indicates. It is not shade tolerant and needs bright sunny conditions to bloom. One major advantage over the popular small street tree, *Cassia surattensis*, is the more open growth habit. This allows the tree to resist winds and be less likely to be blown over, the main problem with *Cassia surattensis*. Expect a height of 10-15 feet with this small tree.

- Origin — Australia
- Foliage — Tiny, dull green compound leaves
- Nutritional requirements — Not fussy, tolerates alkaline soil
- Salt tolerance — Medium
- Drought tolerance — High
- Light requirements — High
- Growth rate — Medium

- Propagation — Seed
- Major problems — None. Attracts egg laying sulphur butterflies. Some newly hatched caterpillars will chew the leaves slightly, but most people consider their attraction a bonus rather than a minus.
- Environmental problems — None
- Availability —Check your local nursery and ask if they can order it for you.

GARDEN NOTES

MARCH GARDEN NOTES

"More than anything, I must have flowers, always, always."
Claude Monet

SILVER TRUMPET
Tabebuia caraiba

GARDENIA
Gardenia jasminoides

APRIL   MAY   JUNE

ROYAL POINCIANA
Delonix regia

APRIL

The list of annuals and vegetables you can plant gets shorter as summer approaches. Annuals include marigolds, amaranthus, asters, marigolds, vincas, zinnias, torenias, portulacas and coleus. Vegetables include sweet potatoes, summer spinach, snap beans, lima beans and southern peas. Warm weather herbs include catnip, sesame, dill, basil, marjoram and lemon verbena. Plant any potted tree, palm, citrus or shrub now — as long as water is available.

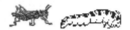

Pests: Spider mites, scales, mealybugs, white flies, and aphids are showing up on new growth. Grasshoppers are also becoming active. You'll also see caterpillars on some plants. Spray with beneficial nematodes now to control lawn grubs, which hatch into maybeetles and attack plant foliage.

As long as rain continues we will not have to water too much. If it stops, resume regular watering until the June wet season begins. **April and Maywhich are normally hot, windy and dry, are the most critical watering months of the year..**

Green Thoughts: Special design problems can cause you to take another look at plants that you might normally ignore. For example, picture a 1-foot planting strip next to a fence that surrounds a pool. No privacy. No room to plant anything. No space for litter or invasive roots. The solution: corn plants (*Dracena*). This old war-horse houseplant will

17

grow to 15 feet outside. It's a narrow grower, has small roots and is relatively neat. An even less expensive option is the aralia hedge, which can be started from cuttings stuck in the ground.

PLANT OF THE MONTH *See color photo on divider*
Silver Trumpet *(Tabebuia caraiba)*

This time of year everyone wants to know the name of the pretty tree with the bright yellow blossoms. The silver trumpet, also known as the yellow tabebuia, is always a traffic stopper when it blooms. The rest of the year the tree, with its twisted gray trunk, might as well be invisible. The yellow tab's beauty is short-lived — it lasts only a few weeks in late March and early April. It can blossom a bit earlier if we have warmer winter weather. A relatively small tree, it reaches about 30 feet in height. The distinctive rough, gray bark provides a good environment for naturalizing orchids and bromeliads. Although it has great beauty, it also has weak wood and is subject to being blown down in storms because of a poor root system. The propensity to blow down, combined with its irregular growth habit makes it a poor choice for a street tree. Locate the tree in a sheltered spot away from winds. A western exposure is best. Try to shelter it by a building or windbreak to the east. It is best used as a lawn tree because flowers drop and cause a mess. The yellow tab is a popular tree that is readily available at most nurseries that sell small trees, or it can be ordered. The Federated Garden Club was instrumental in saving one of Broward County's oldest tabebuias and relocating it to a park where it is blossoming along with twelve other flowering trees representing the various circles that comprise the club. Each tree is identified with its common and botanical name. The park, at the corner of Andrews Avenue and Las Olas Boulevard in Fort Lauderdale, is a good place to visit and see what the flowering tree you select for your property will look like after it has been planted.

- Origin — Paraguay and Argentina
- Foliage — Distinctive silvery green
- Nutritional requirements — Medium
- Salt tolerance — Medium

- Drought tolerance — High
- Light requirements — High
- Growth rate — Medium
- Propagation — Seeds, grafting
- Major problems — None
- Environmental problems — None

GARDEN NOTES

APRIL GARDEN NOTES

"In search of my mother's garden, I found my own."
Alice Walker

APRIL GARDEN NOTES

"And forget not that the earth delights to feel your bare feet and the wind longs to play with your hair."   Kahil Gibran

MAY

May is usually **hot and dry**, which is stressful to new plantings. Tender growth is susceptible to wilt when water is scarce. Large-leafed plants, such as clerodendrum, croton and datura, are among the first to show water stress in the garden. **Base your watering schedule on grass and leaves**. Water when they assume a sharp "V" shape or when large-leafed plants start to wilt. Your garden will tell you when to water.

- **Check irrigation systems for coverage and missing heads**. Prune any branches or foliage that are blocking irrigation. Reliable rains should resume in June.
- This is the month **to get rid of winter annuals**. Replace with marigolds, caladium bulbs, zinnia, coleus, torenia, vinca, portulaca or amaranthus for summer color. Plant **vegetables** such as sweet potato and okra. You can plant any permanent plant in the landscape as long as water is available. Watering is critical with new as well as established plantings. New plants are growing vigorously and need water to avoid wilting. The rains of June are just around the corner.

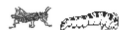

- Lawns are starting to grow rapidly again. **Keep alert for insects** such as chinchbug and armyworm through the summer months. Lots of chewing insects are busy now, including the lubber grasshopper, which loves crinum and spider lilies. Caterpillars and maybeetles do a lot of chewing damage and weevils will notch the leaves of many plants and attack roots. The royal palm bug is also active until June, when rains wash them away. Rain also eliminates aphids, spidermites, thrips and other small sucking insects. Scale and mealybug are becoming more active. Whitefly, snails and slugs are also showing up in large numbers.

- **May is one of the best months for taking cuttings** on woody shrubs such as crotons, ti, dracaena and hibiscus. Grafting and air layering can be done now.

Green Thoughts: If you are re-landscaping, try to group plants that have similar water, environmental and light needs. What makes a plant incompatible with its environment? Basically, it's what it does and does not tolerate. If you live near the ocean, for example, use salt and wind tolerant plants such as Indian hawthorn, spider lily and crinum lily. Sometimes, though, even plants labeled "salt tolerant," such as bougainvillea, oleander and ligustrum, can look fried when they get full exposure to salt winds. Salt tolerant plants usually don't like too much water. Be careful because pittosporum and carissa can get root rot.

PLANT OF THE MONTH
See color photo on divider
Gardenia *(Gardenia jasminoides)*

Gardenia is one of the first plants that new Floridians want to put in their gardens because they remember these fragrant white flowers as corsages and as table decorations. But gardenias are fussy, and many people are disappointed. For best results, plant them in an open flower bed away from house foundations, pools and walkways. They are acid-loving plants, and the high alkalinity near concrete almost guarantees they will have nutritional problems. Most gardenias are big growers and should not be planted close to doorways or in other tight areas. I planted my gardenia from a 3-gallon pot in 1982, and it is now 10 feet tall and 12 feet across. Gardeners who plant them in the wrong places find they have to prune them back. Since they bloom at the ends of the branches, pruning eliminates flowers.

In Florida, gardenias must be grafted if they are planted in the ground because microscopic nematodes can clog up the root system and kill them. They are grafted onto *Gardenia thumbergia*, a nematode-resistant stock.

Look for the main show of flowers from mid-April to mid-May. A scattering of flowers will continue through August if the plants are well fertilized. Fertilize in March, June and October with an ixora/gardenia fertilizer to combat nutritional problems. Try the small growing 'Vetchii' gardenia, which grows to about 4-5 feet and blooms off and on throughout the year. The flowers are much smaller that those on the larger plant, but the fragrance is the same. Big growing varieties include: Miami Supreme, Glazerii, August Beauty and Mystery.

- Origin — China
- Foliage — oval pointed leaves
- Nutritional requirements — Acid fertilizer three times a year
- Soil requirements — Prefers acid soil but can tolerate some alkalinity if fertilized regularly
- Salt tolerance — None
- Drought tolerance — Low
- Light requirements — High to medium
- Growth rate — Moderate
- Propagation — Graftings
- Major problems — Nematodes, chlorotic foliage, sucking insects (such as scale, mealybug and whitefly), thrips (cause flower drop), sooty mold (causes blackened leaves)
- Environmental problems — None
- Availability — Just about any good nursery and many garden centers

GARDEN NOTES

MAY GARDEN NOTES

"The best place to find God is in the garden."
George Bernard Shaw

MAY GARDEN NOTES

"It is forbidden to live in a town which has no greenery."
The Jerusalem Talm

JUNE

- **Fertilize all plantings this month.** Use Lesco 12-2-14 or similar high quality, all-purpose fertilizer on trees, shrubs and palms. Avoid fertilizing citrus because leaf miner likes to feed on the new lush growth. A slower, tougher leaf may be less appealing to the pests. Use Lesco 16-4-8 or similar for lawns. Palms, such as royal, queen, paurotis and pygmy date and cycads such as sago, should be given manganese sulfate to prevent frizzle top. Follow label directions exactly and keep fertilizer off foliage. Sprinkle lightly and evenly; water in.

- If **your lawn** looks terrible right now, don't worry. It should make a comeback now that the rainy season should to have arrived. Once the rains start coming regularly, the lawn will start growing again, and should fill in on its own.

- **If you do not have an irrigation system, this is the most important month of the year to plant**. Choose whatever you like in the shrub, palm, groundcover or tree categories. Nature will do most of the watering for you and eliminate hose dragging if you don't have an irrigation system. Plants will be well established by mid-October when the dry season arrives. Plant virtually anything you want except vegetables and winter annuals. **Select hot weather annuals**, such as marigold, coleus, caladium, vinca, torenia and zinnia. This is also **a great month for air layering, grafting and rooting cuttings**. Many plants will start from shoots stuck in the ground. Water all new plantings daily for the first two weeks if there is no rain. Afterward, water twice a week. Normally, we get good rains in June.

- This is the best time of the year to **cut back hedges and shrubs** if they need it. It is usually not advisable to remove more than one-third of the total green growth of the plant. We have good cloud cover in June, which minimizes sunscald. Plantings that have been hard pruned will re-grow and fill in much quicker now than at any other time of year. Walk around your property and check trees and shrubs that have dead wood, hollow trunks or crossing/rubbing limbs. Slate these for removal before hurricane season gets more active.

- **Bugs are still busy**. Disease can be a problem now. Water only in the morning to avoid mildew on roses and crape myrtle. If plants are close together or growing quickly, open plants up for better air circulation.

Green Thoughts: I applaud the use of palms in the landscape, but I never stop being amazed about what some gardeners do with them. Homeowners regularly use areca palms as foundation plantings and then are surprised when their trees start banging into the eaves. Those who plant queen palms as street trees or in parking lots find that they grow into utility lines and get fried or die from manganese sulfate deficiency, also known as frizzle top.

Cities and homeowners that have queen, royal, pygmy date, paurotis, or sago palms should include an annual application of manganese sulfate in their yearly maintenance budgets.

Most of the small palms are shade-loving because they are understory palms in nature. You can plant these shade-lovers (Cat palm, bamboo palms and parlor palms) fairly close to the house. Unfortunately, few sun-loving palms are small.

PLANT OF THE MONTH *See color photo on divider*
Royal Poinciana *(Delonix regia)*

The royal poinciana symbolizes the beginning of summer with its vivid blooms of orange, red and sometimes yellow. Nothing in the flowering tree world can quite equal a royal poinciana for sheer gaudiness during full bloom.

Proper siting is essential so the full beauty can be displayed and the negatives minimized. The tree's good points include the exquisite flower display, the shade provided by the great umbrella –shaped crown and its hardiness. It does well in sunny, dry locations without baby-sitting.

But these pretty trees do have some negatives – branch and twig drop, messy pods, fine leaves that clog gutters and pool pumps as well as some staining. Shallow roots grab extra water, and lawns and other plantings have a rough time growing under the tree. The tree casts heavy shade in summer and is totally bare for several months during the winter.

Watering may cause leaves to remain on the tree longer, but too much disturbs the bloom cycle, causing a scattering of blooms over a longer period. Irrigated trees may also develop root rot and have decay problems. Pruning must be done carefully as the softwood rots easily.

The royal poinciana is a big tree and needs a large open space so that the full spread of the crown can be accommodated. Expect 40-foot heights and 60-foot –plus horizontal spreads. This is a good tree for highways and unirrigated parks where its beauty can brighten the landscape and care is not routinely provided.

- Origin — Madagascar
- Salt tolerance — Medium
- Foliage — Green and delicate
- Drought tolerance — High
- Growth rate — Fast
- Nutritional requirements — Low
- Propagation — Seed
- Light requirements — High
- Problems — Weak, messy, staining
- Soil requirements — Well drained, not good in heavy soils

"Id rather have roses on my table than diamonds on my neck".
Emma Goldman

JUNE GARDEN NOTES

"The earth laughs in flowers."
Ralph Waldo Emerson

JUNE GARDEN NOTES

"Show me your garden, provided it be your own,
and I will tell you what you are like." **Alfred Austin**

GARDEN NOTES

PINWHEEL JASMINE
Tabernaemontana divaricata

CRAPE MYRTLE
Lagerstroemia indica

BEGONIA *odorata 'Alba'*

Passion vine (*Passiflora incense*) is the host plant for several butterfly species. (Julia, Gulf Frittilary, Zebra). This Zebra longwing (***Heliconius charitonius)*** laying her eggs on the tips of the vine. The vine will become the food source for her newly hatched caterpillars. Butterflies

need both a source of nectar for food and a larval plant on which to lay their eggs. The Zebra longwing was designated **Florida's State Insect** on April 26, 1996 at the request of garden clubs across the state

In 1927, the Florida legislature designated the Mockingbird (Mimus polyglottos) as the state bird. Appropriately attired in a tuxedo, the mockingbird is one of the most impressive entertainers, with the ability to sing songs of at least 30 species of birds as well as mimic the sounds of chattering squirrels, barking dogs, and creaking gates.

9-10". Year-round
Gray with long tail, flashing
white patches on the wings
and tail while in flight

Northern Mockingbird

The mockingbird is omnivorous. It will eat beetles, ants, wasps, grasshoppers, worms, small lizards, fruit and has a fondness for Zebra butterflies!

SEPTEMBER

AUGUST

JULY

JULY

Traditionally the season following an El Nino is ripe for hurricanes. That's what happened in the 1926 hurricane that hit Florida and in 1992 with Hurricane Andrew. **Check your trees now** to minimize possible damage from these devastating storms. **Remove dead wood, crossing limbs, stubs and weak wood** from your trees. When you hire a professional, use only certified arborists.

Bugs are at their height of activity. Mealybugs seem particularly active on jatropha. Be alert for scale, whitefly, mites, thrips, aphids, caterpillars, chinchbug, sod webworms, beetles and weevils.

Make sure your plants are getting enough water. A lot of problems are the result of record-breaking heat and lack of rain. **Check irrigation systems** for broken heads and pipes. Remove water-blocking branches. Use risers to clear taller growing plants. **Water more frequently** so new growth does not wilt
Green Thoughts: Instead of replanting annuals two to three times a year, you can save money by planting perennials. Most perennials give daily color and last longer. I have found that the tall pentas and crossandra can survive at least six to seven years.

PLANT OF THE MONTH *See color photo on divider*
Pinwheel Jasmine *(Tabernaemontana divaricata)*

This is one of the most reliable of the shrub bloomers with a good display of flowers every day of the year. It can grow to 8-10 feet in height but is a slow grower. The pinwheel jasmine does well in sun or shade but cannot tolerate high alkalinity. Do not plant this beauty within 5-6 feet of any cement including house foundations. The plant should be used as a specimen. It is excellent for lighting up a shady corner or located near an area used for night entertaining. The pinwheel jasmine has a layered growth habit and can make an interesting specimen for an oriental garden. White pinwheel-like blooms are individually small but are carried in enough quantity to make a good display. Fertilize with an ixora/gardenia fertilizer in March, June and October.

- Origin — India
- Foliage — Glossy oval pointed leaves.
- Growth rate — Slow to medium
- Nutritional requirements — Must have an acid soil or acid type fertilizer to do well.
- Soil requirements — Acid soil
- Salt tolerance — Low
- Drought tolerance — Low
- Light requirements — Wide
- Propagation — Cuttings
- Major problems — Mealybug, scale, mites, nematodes.
- Environmental problems — None

GARDEN NOTES

JULY GARDEN NOTES

"Oh, this is the joy of the rose
That it blooms,
And goes."
Willa Cather

JULY GARDEN NOTES

"Ah, summer, what power you have to make us suffer and like it."
Russell Baker

GARDEN NOTES

AUGUST

Plant any tree, shrub, palm or groundcover. Vegetables are limited to cherry tomato, pepper and okra. Annuals tolerant of heat include amaranthus, torenia, vinca, zinnia, coleus, cosmos and marigold. **Keep mulch 1-2 inches away from all plant stems.**

Inspect trees at the beginning of the month for pruning work. **August, September and October are the big hurricane months** with the peak of the season activity on Sept.10. **Cut back poinsettias** before the end of August for the last time in order to ensure good winter color.

Weeds and insects typically go crazy this month. Chinchbugs, scale, mealybugs, thrips, caterpillars, sod webworms, etc. are on the prowl. Co-exist with them unless damage gets to unacceptable levels. **Chinchbugs** can be detected by pouring soapy water where good and bad grass meet. After pouring the water, observe the grass for a few minutes. Chinchbugs and other insects will come to the surface. Adults are small black insects with white patches on the wings. Use Dursban around the bad grass patch in a band about 4 feet wide. Citrus, croton, avocado and mango are susceptible to **spider mites and thrips**. Discourage them with a strong jet of water from a hose directed to the undersides of the leaves. Hibiscus, citrus, palms, gardenia and ixora are susceptible to **scale and mealybug**. Treat with Orthene or Safer's insecticidal soap

Green Thoughts: We all have planted the wrong tree in the wrong place -- too wide, too tall, too bare. But when a tree grows into

power lines, the electric company. sends its crews to clear the lines. Ugly V-shaped or one-sided trees are often the result. Get smart and order **"Plant the Right Tree in the Right Place,"** a free booklet from Florida Power & Light Co. To order, call 305-442-8770 in Dade County, 954-797-5000 in Broward County, 561-697-8000 in Palm Beach County.

PLANT OF THE MONTH *See color photo on divider*
Crape Myrtle (*Lagerstroemia indica*)

Crape myrtle is a longtime favorite with southern gardeners. The big clusters of bloom remind us of lilacs in the North. The large trusses come in pink, red, white, and purple shades as well as bicolor. Most of the flowers are not fragrant, but a few hybrids like 'Natchez' have a pleasing light odor. Bloom period is from May to October. These large shrubs or small trees grow to 20 feet and are multiseason plants that offer showy flowers, attractive bark, red to yellow fall leaf color and an interesting growth habit. All this would be plenty for the average gardener, but South Floridians demand year-round foliage. Unfortunately, crape myrtles are semi-bare from January to April. They leaf out very late in the spring, and sometimes people think they are dead. Remember this before you dig the plants out. Think carefully where you place the crape myrtle because of its deciduous nature. Queen crape myrtle is a similar but much larger and more tropical relative. The most common flower color is purple, but a nice pink form is sometimes seen. The tree can grow to 30 feet or more, and the big leaves turn an attractive red in late fall. It is deciduous for a shorter time than the regular crape myrtle but does not flower as long. Bloom time is usually from May to September. If you are growing the regular crape myrtle, try to use the national arboretum selections from Washington, D.C. They have Indian names and are resistant to powdery mildew, a fungal disease that ruins the flowers and affects the foliage. These selections often have a longer blooming period than others on the market. Names to look for include Acoma, Biloxi, Comanche, Hopi, Lipan, Miami, Muskogee, Natchez, Osage, Sioux, Tuskegee, Yuma and Zuni.
- Origin — Southern Asia and Australia
- Foliage — Oval pointed green leaves

- Growth rate — Medium
- Nutritional requirements — Not fussy
- Soil requirements — Wide
- Salt tolerance — Low
- Drought tolerance — High
- Light requirements — High
- Propagation — Seed
- Major problems — Powdery mildew, root rot, aphids
- Environmental problems — None

GARDEN NOTES

AUGUST GARDEN NOTES

"Flowers are sunshine, food and medicine to the soul."
Luther Burbank

AUGUST GARDEN NOTES

"Nothing is more completely the child of art than a garden."
Sir Walter Scott

GARDEN NOTES

SEPTEMBER

We are in the **height of hurricane season** right now. The tropics
have heated up and so should your pruning. **Check the trees and
shrubs** in your yard one final time. Cut away dead wood and
remove crossing limbs and branches that overhang the house

- Weeds continue to proliferate. Evenings are starting to cool, so
  it is more comfortable working in the garden. **Continue to
  mulch** but keep it 1-2 inches from the stems of all plants.

- Continue to **patrol the garden , checking for pests**. Mealybugs and scale have been abundant the past few years. Check
  lawns for chinch bug, armyworm and sod webworm. A garden
  with many kinds of plants has fewer pests than gardens with
  lots of mass plantings. Avoid insect magnets like oleander,
  which require constant spraying.

- **You can still take cuttings and divide perennials** but do it as
  soon as possible. Days are getting shorter and less sunlight
  signals the plants to slow down their growth. Cuttings will not
  root as quickly.

- If you do not have sprinklers, **plant by Sept. 15** so the new
  plantings will have time to settle in before the dry season
  resumes around October 15.
- **Check irrigation systems** for broken heads and pipes.

- **Consider starting vegetables and annuals from seed**. Try salvia, verbena, ageratum, celosia, nasturtium and wax begonia along with vegetable varieties of lettuce, lima beans, tomato, onion, cabbage and broccoli. Protect tender seedlings from heavy September rains

- Winter annuals will be available at about the end of this month. **Continue planting all trees and shrubs**, but be sure to water them if no irrigation is available.

Green Thoughts: If you have windows vulnerable to break-ins, install security plantings with nasty thorns. Some of the big landscape bromeliads are spiny and do well in sun or shade. Pereskia, crown of thorns, and various agaves and dwarf yuccas have spiny or pointed leaves and stems and like full sun. Carissa and silverthorn make good hedge plantings and do well in sun or shade.

PLANT OF THE MONTH *See color photo on divider*
Begonia *odorata 'Alba'*

This begonia has been around the Florida landscape for a number of years. It was used mostly in hanging baskets in the past. It is an amazingly good high ground cover for part shade locations. This begonia will reach about 3 feet in height and is easy to propagate from cuttings. It is in bloom year round compared to many begonias which bloom only in late winter or spring. The flowers produce a nice cascading informal display of white through the year and are lightly fragrant. It can be used under windows or in front of taller shrubbery. I think this is one of the best perennials around.

- Origin — Jamaica
- Foliage — Rounded glossy coarse foliage

- Growth rate — Fast
- Nutritional requirements — Medium
- Soil requirements — Not fussy except for overly wet or dry conditions.
- Salt tolerance — Low
- Drought tolerance — Low
- Light requirements — Part shade
- Propagation — Cuttings
- Major problems — Root rot
- Environmental problems — None

GARDEN NOTES

SEPTEMBER GARDEN NOTES

"There is no gardening without humility. Nature is constantly sending even its oldest scholars to the bottom of the class for some egregious blunder."
Alfred Austin

SEPTEMBER GARDEN NOTES

"I am spending delightful afternoons in my garden watering everything living around me. As I grow older, I feel everything departing and I love everything with more passion."
Emile Zola

RED JATROPHA
Jatropha integerrima 'Compacta'

WHITE IXORA
'Frankie Hipp' Ixora,
Ixora 'Frankie Hipp'

BABY SUNROSE
a heat tolerant plant

YELLOW ELDER
Tecoma stans

A **Gulf Frittilary**
collects nectar from **Blue Porterweed**

DECEMBER   NOVEMBER   OCTOBER

OCTOBER

Vegetable gardening hits high gear by mid-month when the first refreshing cool fronts start to penetrate the peninsula on a regular basis. Vegetable choices include broccoli, turnips, spinach, onions, carrots, cauliflower, beets, radishes, mustard, cabbage, lettuce, tomatoes, potatoes, parsley, celery, peas, summer squash and lima and snap beans. Most **herbs** should be planted out now. Strawberries also can be planted. **Annuals** include: coleus, marigold, torenia, vinca, impatiens, salvia, portulaca, cosmos, ageratum, gloriosa daisy, celosia, verbena, wax begonia, calendula, alyssum, snapdragon, nasturtium, hollyhock, cornflower, pansy, candytuft and larkspur.

The last big fertilization of the year should be applied to all plants this month. A high quality all-purpose fertilizer should be fine for most trees. I have used Lesco 12-2-14 with good success on most plantings. Lawns benefit from a good application of Lesco 16-4-8. But any good quality fertilizer with trace elements should do the job. Apply lightly and evenly and water in after application.

The dry season begins mid-month. As soon as you can, it's a good idea to check irrigation systems before their winter workouts. Fungal problems appear with the cooler weather, so make sure watering is restricted to the morning hours between 2 and 10 a.m. The dry season will last through May, so some supplemental irrigation will be necessary for lawns and bedding plants.

Insects are still with us, but populations will fall as the cooler weather arrives. We never get a complete break like the winter-bound folks in the north. Caterpillars will be active on cassia, oleander and bougainvillea. Mites, thrips, scale, army and sod webworms will be active. Check for infestations once a week.

Green Thoughts: Fort Lauderdale's Riverland Civic Association has planted about 500 flowering trees throughout their neighborhood in recent years. Now Fort Lauderdale jail inmates are going to plant another 150 flowering trees in the neighborhood. Ten inmates overseen by two correction officers planted the new trees. The city's Adopt-A-Tree program provided the trees. This is the best program I have heard of in recent years. The city will certainly be a more beautiful place as the trees mature and start to bloom on a regular basis.

PLANT OF THE MONTH *See color photo on divider*
Red Jatropha (*Jatropha interrima)*

I often think how quickly we become jaded by the flower displays in south Florida. We forget how lucky we are compared to our northern neighbors. Jatropha, or perigrina is one of our most dependable bloomers in the small tree or large shrub category. It blooms reliably every day of the year. This plant has red flowers that appear at the end of every branch. Blooms are not large, but they make a decent permanent scattering of flowers over the entire plant.

The standard species plant is very open-growing and is good for a landscape where a small see-through tree is needed. This see-through characteristic is an excellent quality if you are designing a landscape with security in mind. The 'Compacta' form is much tighter in growth habit and tops out in the 8 to 10 foot range. Most people will opt for the compact form.

Jatropha is relatively free of pests, but attacks by scale, mealybug and leaf miner are not unknown. Damage is usually temporary, and new leaf growth quickly follows. This plant is a must as a butterfly attractant and usually has many types flocking around. Hummingbirds are winter visitors.

I suspect we may see more color forms of perigrina as time goes on. I have seen a pink form at some of the collector nurseries, but it is very hard to find.
- Origin — Cuba

- Foliage — Variable dark green leaves, some lobed and others oval and pointed
- Growth rate — Medium
- Nutritional requirements — Low
- Soil requirements — Wide
- Salt tolerance — Medium
- Drought tolerance — High
- Light requirements —High
- Propagation — Seed, Cuttings
- Environmental problems — None

GARDEN NOTES

OCTOBER GARDEN NOTES

"If you want to be happy for an hour, have a party.
If you want to be happy for a week, kill a pig and eat it...But if
you want to be happy all your life,
become a gardener."
Old Chinese Saying

OCTOBER GARDEN NOTES

*"You cannot perceive beauty
but with a serene mind."*
Henry David Thoreau

NOVEMBER

Plant - The dry season has begun with cooler temperatures and less rainfall. November is like spring and gardeners enjoy a resurgence of interest and energy in the garden. **Fall plant installation is fine for virtually all plantings as long as we have sufficient rainfall**. The **vegetable list** includes tomato, endive, escarole, snap bean, potato, pepper, pea, lima bean, collards, parsley, potato, celery, turnip, mustard, onion, spinach, lettuce, radish, cabbage, beet, carrot and broccoli. The **annual list** is also large and includes sweet pea, verbena, pansy, hollyhock, alyssum, wax begonia, candytuft, calendula, baby's breath, nasturtium, snapdragon, marigold, coleus, vinca, torenia, impatiens, gloriosa daisy, salvia, portulaca, cosmos, ageratum, and celosia. Strawberries can be planted now.

Bloom - Many flowering shrubs and trees will start to bloom now that the dry weather has begun. Look for good bloom displays on cassias, orchid trees, floss silk trees, dombeya, and yesterday-today-and-tomorrow, Chinese hat plant, bougainvillea, clock bush and other favorites that put on a good show in the cooler weather.

Irrigation - The dry season has begun and will last through May. Check the irrigation system for broken pipes, blown heads and other maintenance problems. Prune back exuberant summer growth that may have covered heads so coverage is not complete. Put heads on risers if the water spray is buried in the shrubbery. Plant impatiens in bonsai pots so the rest of the yard is not overwatered to the point of root rot on permanent plantings.

Disease - Problems increase with cooler weather and heavy dew. It is critical to adjust sprinklers to water in the morning only to avoid fungal leaf spotting on lawns and some shrubbery. Watering any time between 2-10 a.m. minimizes fungal problems.

Upgrades - Consider upgrading the landscape for your own enjoyment. Landscaping is a flexible thing that changes with the stages of your family's growth and needs. That former play yard may function now as an herb or rose garden. Maybe you want to incorporate a water feature near your patio. The sky is the limit based on your interest, energy and money.

Insects - Insect populations gradually are reduced as the cooler, drier weather begins. Spider mite damage can show up, particularly on plantings located under building eaves. Slugs, snails and cutworms are active some years. The Cuban May beetle will lay eggs,which will hatch out as white grubs to eat grass roots. Some caterpillars, mealybug and scale are still causing landscape problems.

Green Thoughts: Community entryways should receive extra attention as they set the tone for the residences within. Many considerations are involved such as utilities above and below ground, sight lines for vehicles, heavy pedestrian traffic and the soil type and growing conditions for the selected plants. These plantings may not be irrigated so only the toughest should be planted. Spider lilies used in medians in Fort Lauderdale have done well. Ruellias, crinum lilies, cardboard palm, Fakahatchee grass, and others offer the promise of minimum maintenance for the entry landscape.

PLANT OF THE MONTH *See color photo on divider*
White Ixora, *Ixora 'Frankie Hipp'*

I noticed this white ixora mixed in with the pink 'Nora Grant' ixora at the one of the nurseries where I conduct my plant clinics. I have not seen many white ixora so this caught my attention. It is a hybrid and a white form of the 'Nora Grant' that is so popular in landscaping. I like white as a color in landscaping. It is particularly effective with night lighting for evening entertaining. If this ixora is as prolific a bloomer as the 'Nora Grant', it should be a knockout. Growers report a light fragrance at night which is another asset. This is a good grower capable of attaining 6-8 feet under good conditions. Remember that ixoras and other plants bloom at the branch tips. Do not use the plant as a hedge as you will cut off all the flowers, defeating the whole purpose. I see this plant serving nicely as a background or screening plant allowed to grow naturally. These ixoras are not impressive for the first year or two but fill in nicely as they age. The 'Nora Grant' association brings another benefit, which is good resistance to nematodes. The root knot nematode is deadly to several ixoras although it may take a few years to kill it. The 'Maui' ixora is extremely subject to nematode damage and lasts only three to four years in the land-scape. The Taiwan Dwarf ixoras have similar problems and are very cold sensitive.

Sources: You can have your local nursery order it for you from a wholesale grower.

- Origin: S. E. Asia
- Foliage: Glossy oval pointed dark green leaves.
- Growth rate: Moderate
- Nutritional requirements: Acid fertilizer in March, June and October. Keep away from cement (ideally 4-5 feet) to minimize this problem.
- Soil requirements: Acid preferred
- Salt tolerance: Medium
- Drought tolerance: Medium
- Light requirement: Medium to high
- Propagation: Cuttings
- Major problems: Scale, mealybugs, leaf spotting, chlorosis from excess alkalinity
- Environmental problem: None

NOVEMBER GARDEN NOTES

"A morning glory at my window satsfies me more than the metaphysics of books."
Walt Whitman

NOVEMBER GARDEN NOTES

"No occupation is so delightful to me as the culture of the earth...and no culture comparable to that of the garden...But though an old man, I am but a young gardener."

Thomas Jefferson

GARDEN NOTES

 **DECEMBER**

Winter sets in this month and **a freeze is possible.** Forecasts can vary greatly from the coast to the inland suburbs. I remember a time back in the early 1980s when it was 35 degrees at the Fort Lauderdale airport (about a mile from the coast), 27 degrees in Davie at the IFAS Research Center (about 10 miles from the coast) and 19 degrees along Highway 27 (about 20 miles west of the coast).

Stay with the hardier type plants in inland locations such as wax myrtle, dahoon holly or native red maple. If a freeze threatens, cover tender plants with a sheet, box or blanket. **Do not use clear plastic. Water heavily** the night the freeze is expected and **pull mulch away from the plants**. The warm soil will release heat and raise the temperature around the low plantings and could save them.

Plant poinsettia. After the holiday cut to 12" - 18". We will remind you to cut again in May and over the summer. For holiday blooms, **no cuts after September!** Think of your holiday poinsettia plant like it's your Christmas tree. Chances are good that you wouldn't tear a branch off the holiday tree and start munching on it. Likewise, with the poinsettia. Experts say if your child or pet ate 10 or 12 poinsettia leaves they might get sick, but that's highly unlikely. Researchers at Ohio University found that a 50-pound child would have to eat more than 1.25 **pounds** of poinsettia bracts (about500 to 600 leaves) to exceed the experimental doses.

You can **plant vegetables** now — lima and snap beans, cauliflower, eggplant, turnips, tomatoes, spinach, peas, celery, radishes, onions, cabbage, beets, carrots, Chinese cabbage, broccoli and lettuce.

Many **annuals can be added to the garden** —torenia, coleus, marigold, vinca, impatiens, cosmos, ageratum, celosia, portulaca, salvia, gloriosa daisy, nasturtium, alyssum, cornflower, pansy, petunia, dianthus, wax begonia, hollyhock, verbena, sweetpea, larkspur and calendula.

This is a good month to **plant roses**, or transplant anything hardy. Any woody plant can be installed now if you have an adequate water supply to irrigate until the wet season begins in June. **When transplanting trees**: Water first, then dig the root ball 18 inches deep and 1 foot wide per inch of trunk. **Citrus**: Leave unripened fruit on the tree. Flavor does not improve once it is picked. **Succulents**: Guard against overwatering. This is their dormant season and overwatering can induce rot

Check irrigation systems frequently. **Water about twice a week if there is no rain.**
New growth has slowed down or is hardened off and some pests may go dormant. But **keep alert for spider mites and thrips**, which can do a lot of damage to crotons, avocados, mangoes, copperleaf and some citrus. These sucking insects attack the leaves, causing a stippling pattern and a brown spot in the center of the leaves.

PLANT OF THE MONTH *See color photo on divider*
Yellow elder (*Tecoma stans*)

The yellow elder is bright and cheerful from October to December. It sometimes blooms in the spring with showy yellow trumpets up to 2 inches long that are borne in big clusters. Yellow elder is drought- and neglect-tolerant and makes a bushy tree that grows to 20 feet. However, there's one drawback: The long seed pods carried through the winter are somewhat messy. Dr. Derek Burch, a horticultural consultant from Plantation that consults with commercial nurseries, introduced a tree, *Tecoma stans* 'Burchii', that blooms throughout the year.
- Origin — Caribbean region
- Foliage — Leaves pinnately compound, light green and semi-evergreen
- Salt tolerance — Medium

- Drought tolerance — High
- Light requirements — Needs sun to partial shade
- Growth rate — Fast
- Disadvantages — Can seed excessively
- Major problems — None
- Nutritional requirements — Low, can do without fertilizer. Use 6-6-6 or whatever you have on hand.

GARDEN NOTES

DECEMBER GARDEN NOTES

"Never give up listening to the sounds of birds."
John James Audubon

DECEMBER GARDEN NOTES

"For in the true nature of things, if we will consider, every green tree is far more glorious than if it were made of gold and silver."
Martin Luther

Vines

Allamanda Vine

**Petrea
(Queens Wreath,
Florida Wisteria)
graces an archway**

Cobalt Clitoria

Golden Dewdrop and Hamelia Patens attract butterflies and birds.

A simple clay saucer filled with fresh food or water will bring Blue Jays and other species to your yard.

Milkweed is a favorite of the Monarch butterfly

ANSWERS TO
THE FREQUENTLY ASKED QUESTIONS ABOUT:

ACCENT PLANTS

Q. I need a **focal point** for my garden. What are some dramatic plants that I might use?

A. **Heliconias and bird of paradise** are among our most architectural plants. Spectacular blooms and foliage are trademarks with these perennials. **Heliconias** come in varying sizes from 2-3 foot dwarfs to giants almost 20 feet in height. Some heliconias are running types and others make slowly spreading clumps. Flowers vary in conformation, but are spectacular – generally in the orange, red or yellow color range. Visit Flamingo Gardens in Davie to see the different types available. They also host Heliconia Society plant sales from time to time. Shade or part shade and good moisture levels are essential for heliconias. They make spectacular flower arrangements, as do bird of paradise. Some flowers can last as long as three weeks in arrangements.

Birds of paradise includes the giant white bird of paradise with blue and white flowers to 25 feet tall and 20 feet across, and the orange and blue bird of paradise to 6 feet tall, 6 feet wide that we are more familiar with. Birds of paradise like sun to partial shade and a medium to dry location. A lot of organic material or mulch is appreciated by all of these plants. The orange bird of paradise is often a shy bloomer. An azalea/gardenia fertilizer, will encourage bloom.

Q. I live in the western part of Broward County and have planted a **white bird of paradise** in my yard. What is the **best way to trim it** when the fronds get torn up by wind?

A. White bird of paradise is cold sensitive and you are pretty far west for it to be considered a major permanent accent plant. It will suffer from cold every few years that far west. Enjoy it while the warm weather is with us. Use lopping shears or a good saw (the Felco is superb) to cut off old leaf stubs to the base or trunk of the plant.

Q. I have a **bird of paradise** that gets water daily from the sprinkler system nearby. **It has a fungus** but I sprayed it with a fungicide. Is there any more I can do?

A. Your bird of paradise is being drowned under your present watering regime. Spraying copper fungicide is good but won't be effective with your overwatering schedule. Bird of paradise likes sunny dry conditions. It comes from South Africa where the plants receive 20-30 inches of rain yearly at most. We get 50-60 inches of rain before we turn on the sprinklers. During the rainy season turn the sprinklers off unless the plants indicate a need (wilting). You might consider half or three-quarter heads to keep your bird of paradise dry when other plants are getting irrigated. If it is crowded in with other plants consider moving it to an area with better air movement to minimize fungus.

Q. The leaves of my two **bird of paradise** plants have curled up. What should I do?

A. They are in water stress. Water right away.

Q. Can I plant **bird of paradise under my queen palms**?

A. Bird of paradise and queen palms are generally quite compatible. They both like sun and dry conditions. Give your queen palm an annual treatment of manganese sulfate; it won't hurt the bird of paradise either. I would use azalea/gardenia fertilizer on the bird of paradise. Bird of paradise has a reputation for being a slow starter. We have received numerous success stories from owners whose plants were six or more years old that were performing beautifully. Generous fertilizing and maturity makes all the difference with these plants.

Q. Can I grow **pampas grass** from seed in South Florida?

A. Pampas grass grows in south Florida, but usually seems to decline here. It looks much better from central Florida north. We probably are a bit too far south to grow it well. The beautiful plumes you see are from female plants. The male plants do not put up pretty seed panicles. Pampas grass is grown from seed, so you do not necessarily know if you are getting a male or a female plant until it blooms. The plumes appear in the summer and fall here. The plant is green year around. Cut it back to about 1 to 2 feet in height in late January or February for fresh new foliage. The leaves are like razors, so wear a long sleeve shirt and gloves when working with it. Add about 50% peat moss to the existing soil to encourage moisture retention if you are on sandy soil. Give pampas grass full sun.

ANNUALS

Q. What are some **annuals that can tolerate the summer heat**?
A. Celosia (cockscomb), gallardia (blanket flower), gomphrena (globe amaranth), African marigold (*Tagetes erecta*), portulaca, torenia, zinnia, and verbena are annuals that can tolerate heat. For a low splash of color comparable to impatiens and wax begonias, the verbena would come the closest. All summer annuals suffer to some extent as heat, humidity and insect populations are at their height during the season.

Q. What **all-around fertilizer** can I use for my annuals?
A. You can get by with a monthly fertilization with Peters 20-20-20 liquid soluble fertilizer or one application of Dynamite. Water annuals about twice a week after they are established.

Q. What do commercial seed growers do for **good germination of seeds**? The seeds collected in my yard, mainly marigolds, do not have a high rate of germination.
A. Most annuals from seeds nowadays are hybrids or tetraploids. They often are either sterile or produce only a little viable seed. For best germination, you would have to specify old varieties that have not been so highly bred. Your germination rate should be better then. Marigolds are best germinated in an indirect light location – the north side of the house under a shade tree. After that they can be gradually moved out to a full sun location. Seedlings may suffer from damping off, which is a fungal condition that causes them to collapse from rot at the base of the stem. Keep seedlings in an area where there is good air movement.

Q. Where can I get **seeds for ornamental cabbage and New Guinea impatiens**?

A. Ornamental cabbage should grow here in the coolest part of the year between December and March. Seeds for ornamental cabbage and New Guinea impatiens, a more sun-tolerant variety of impatiens, are available through Parks Seed (See Supplier's list).

Q. What can I **plant under a silk oak tree**? I was considering impatiens.
A. I would not damage the feeder roots of the silk oak for impatiens. Consider using a more permanent plant like pentas, which will last about three years in the ground and is more aggressive and larger than impatiens. It blooms all the time and is a durable cut flower lasting a week or more in water. The silk oak likes dry conditions and impatiens needs a lot of water, so it is important to choose this planting to avoid root rot on the silk oak.

Q. I am having **trouble with my impatiens**, which I purchased from different shops. They seem to die overnight and the bottoms come off. What care do they require?
A. Your soil is infected with a fungal disease, which is killing the plants. Treat the soil with Subdue; it may bring some relief, but there is no guarantee. The plants also may have been infected at the nursery. Impatiens are annuals planted in October and finishing up in April and May. They need shade for an extended growing season. They use a lot of water and excessive water can cause root rot and kill permanent plantings. Plant the impatiens in a large bonsai pot with sterilized soil.

Q. What ideas do you have to **replace impatiens as bedding plants**?
A. For your bedding plants, substitute something like wax begonia and red salvia for winter and torenia and marigolds for summer, which need watering only about twice a week instead of daily. "New Look" pentas and purple weeping salvia are new perennials that show good promise.

Q. My garden up north had **dusty miller**. Can I plant it here?
A. Dusty miller is a variety of artemesia with beautiful silvery foliage. The summer heat and rainfall can do them in, particularly if an irrigation system is nearby. They like a sunny, well-drained location where they will not receive a lot of water. They are used as

bedding plants or a border. The silvery leaves contrast beautifully with pink geraniums, which like similar growing conditions. They also look good with yellow or red blooms. I would treat them as annuals here. Plant in October and figure them to fade away by May. If you can plant them in a raised bed with good drainage they may go over the summer. Dusty miller is salt tolerant and a nice accent for oceanfront condominiums. The form we grow here is sencio.

Q. How do we care for **portulaca**?
A. Portulacas are summer annuals that like sunny dry locations. In wet years they are much more likely to get leggy and rot. The **Purslane** is similar and lasts longer in the landscape under dry conditions.

Q. I planted periwinkles, New Guinea impatiens and other annuals, spread a layer of mulch and have watered them diligently but **they are dying**. What did I do wrong?
A. Overwatering causes periwinkles to die from fungal disease. Once established they do not want any extra water. The New Guinea impatiens can tolerate more sun than the regular impatiens, but they are still delicate.

Q. Can I plant castor bean in South Florida?
A. **The red-leafed castor plant**, which has poisonous seeds, sometimes is used as a bedding plant in Europe because of the tropical foliage. Grow it if you like but consider it weedy and a bit dangerous.

Q. My **globe amaranth** has eggs on it from a fly-like insect. The plants seem to die off. What is happening?
A. The globe amaranth is a summer annual that will fade at the end of the wet season in October. I would remove the plants. I suspect your insect is a stem borer, which is hard to control with a conventional spray. It can also attack marigolds

BROMELIADS, ORCHIDS & EPIPHYTES

One of the great advantages to living in central or south Florida is the opportunity to experiment with orchids. These exotic plants are considered by many to be difficult and only suitable for experts and collectors. There are some that fit into those categories but many orchids are quite easy and do not require excess fussing. I always consider myself the ultimate lazy gardener and have naturalized many cattleyas, oncidiums and dendrobiums on the branches of open- growing rough-barked trees, which provide a perfect natural habitat. Nylon stockings or old pantyhose are perfect for attaching the orchid into the crotch of a tree. The nylon rots in about a year and the orchid should be fairly well attached by that time. I do not feed any of the orchids and have some irrigation heads on risers so that most of the orchids get watered when the sprinklers water the rest of the yard. It is fun to look up in the trees and get a surprise when an orchid comes into bloom. The only disadvantage is that they cannot be brought into the house unless you cut them.

The **cattleyas** are the traditional corsage orchid that most people know. They often are fragrant and definitely are spectacular in bloom. Most flower only one time a year at a specific time. You could create an "orchid" tree by buying a different cattleya for each month of the year and attaching it to a suitable tree. The color range is incredible with white, yellow and purple predominating. These orchids are from the tropical Americas and enjoy a medium shade.

I like the **dendrobiums** as another easy orchid. They come from Southeast Asia and Australia. They take brighter light than the cattleyas and go dormant during the cooler weather. Hold off on feeding and watering during the winter months. Purple and white are dominant colors. The flowers are carried on spikes and are much smaller than the cattleyas but still make a nice show. They can bloom several times a year.

Oncidiums are good bloomers with yellow flowers predominating. Their airy spikes of bloom can extend for several feet above the plant. I have only the common yellow type that blooms for me in the spring. I have seen them in bloom at other times of the year but this may be a species variation.

I consider the other common species a bit more challenging for the beginner. **Vanda** orchids originate in Southeast Asia and need full sun, hot weather and daily watering. They also benefit from frequent applications of fertilizer. My yard is too shady and the daily watering regime is too much work for me to try vandas. These plants have long exposed hanging roots and spectacular blooms. Some vandas bloom all year, which is a big plus. The hanging roots seem awkward in a hanging basket but are very effective when attached to the trunk of a water-tolerant palm in full sun.

Phalaenopsis like cooler weather and usually are winter bloomers. These moth orchids have incredibly long lasting flowers with bloom spikes effective for three to four months. White is a predominant color and very effective at night. They like bright shade, constant moisture and lots of fertilizer. Many people do well with these plants, which also originate in Southeast Asia.

The **paphiopedilum** orchids have a superficial resemblance to ladies slipper orchids up north, and are commonly called ladies slippers here. They like watering every day and medium light. The spotted leaves are quite attractive and add to their beauty. These orchids also come from Southeast Asia.

This is a tiny sampling of what is available to the orchid grower. I think these plants have the same magic as roses and once hooked you will come back again and again.

Botanical gardens give excellent classes on orchids from time to time. There are several orchid societies that meet monthly with programs and plant sales. The county agents office has a brochure available on orchids.

There are a number of specialty books on orchids and bromeliads available at Fairchild Tropical Gardens Book Store in

Coral Gables. This is one of the best horticultural bookstores in South Florida that I have found. County libraries also have books available.

Q. Will a **pineapple plant** get big here? How should I plant and care for it?

A. Pineapple plants can be started from the tops of fruit that you buy. Cut the top off with the leaves and place in a sunny, dry spot. Pineapples like full sun and sharp draining soil. Mealybugs and nematodes are the main problems. Safer's insecticidal soap will take care of the cotton-like mealybugs. Use organic matter in your soil to repel nematodes. Aged cypress mulch is a good choice – mix it about 50/50 with the existing soil. Fertilize with a granular 7-3-7 fertilizer with minor elements of magnesium and iron, in March, June, October and December. Propagation is by suckers, which arise from the axils of the leaves, and slips, which occur on the stalk below the fruit. Plant in early summer for quick establishment. Space about 15 inches apart to allow for spreading. The plant is a bromeliad and may grow 18-24 inches tall. It takes about two years to get fruit.

Q. How can I **make my orchids bloom**? They are on an east porch that receives sun until 10 a.m. They are watered and fertilized weekly with Schultz 19-31-17. What do you suggest?

A. Orchids such as vandas and dendrobiums like a lot of light. Cattleyas are moderate in light requirements, and phalaenopsis want only filtered light. If the plants are not mature, they will not bloom.

Q. I received an orchid as a gift. It has round pencil-like leaves and long roots hanging in a cypress wood basket. How should I care for it?

A. Your orchid is probably a **vanda** type, which usually like almost full sun. Use orchid fertilizer about once a week, and water daily.

Q. My **cattleya** orchid looks as if it's going to bloom and then it doesn't. What's wrong?

A. Try feeding your cattleya monthly with Peters 20-20-20 to encourage growth and bloom.

Q. I have **"airplants" and Spanish moss** in my trees. Are they parasites and will they hurt the tree?
A. The "airplants" in your trees are various types of bromeliads. Many of these have attractive red, yellow or blue flowers in the spring season. They grow in oak and cypress trees and are native to Florida. Bromeliads are not parasites and do not damage the oak trees. I would leave them alone. You may also have native orchids in your trees if you are lucky.

Q. Can you tell me how to **ship "airplants" to another state**? What care to they require?
A. Law protects all native "airplants" or bromeliads. They have to be collected by a commercial native plant nursery that is licensed to collect and propagate. The plants need phyto-sanitary inspection for diseases and insects before they can be shipped out of state. The rules are even tougher for export. It's a lot of work. I suggest buying exotic bromeliads, which are showier than the natives. Look up the local telephone number for the Division of Plant Industry under Florida State of: Department of Agriculture and Consumer Services. Inspection agents are usually at the phone from 8-8:30 a.m. and from 4-4:30 p.m.; at other times, leave a recorded message. Call 352-372-3505 in Gainesville for inspection forms, etc. "Airplants" require high humidity and a light feeding monthly with a liquid fertilizer such as Peters 20-20-20.

Q. Can you give me information on **how to attach plants such as orchids and bromeliads to trees** without nails and wire?
A. Twine that naturally decays within a year does the job nicely and so will old nylon stockings or pantyhose. Tie the orchids or bromeliads into the crotch of the tree, and they will attach naturally within the year. Choose a rough-barked, open-growing tree like live oak or *Lysiloma sabicu* for excellent results. Palms like the date, Canary Island date and tall veitchias are good for sun loving vanda orchids. Place the orchids higher than 7 feet so they won't be stolen. You are replicating nature and the plants seem healthier than some grown in fancy orchid houses with fungal problems.

Q. **Should I pot my bromeliads**?
A. I don't like plants in pots and use my bromeliads as ground

covers. When the pups are almost as large as the mother plant you can break them off at the base where the plants join and set them out in the soil. Potting soil for bromeliads should be light and free draining and contain a good deal of organic matter.

Q. I have a **'Fireball' bromeliad**. How do I care for it?
A. These plants like bright light and show better color in the sun. This bromeliad grows with roots that connect to each other. You can cut off an individual or several bromeliad whorls (a circle of three or more rosettes of leaves at one node) and plant them in a clay pot with an orchid or cactus mix. Keep the plant in a morning sun location and keep the center of the cup filled with water.

Q. I acquired a *Vriesa splendens* or **flaming sword** with green/pink leaves. I have located the plant where it gets no direct sunlight. The directions say to water during the rest of the growing season and keep relatively dry during the rest of the year. **When is the growing season**?
A. Give your plant one to two hours of morning sun to restore the color to the leaves. The main growing season here is from May-October although the plant would be growing more slowly during the dry season. Water less in the November-April period.

Q. **My bromeliads** have made babies. **When do I cut them off from the mother plant**? Where do I plant them?
A. Bromeliads generally like shady spots although some varieties will grow in full sun. Cut the babies off when they are one third the size of the mother plant. The mother plant dies after blooming and the babies take over, forming a clump. You can leave them as a clump or cut the babies apart and plant in the ground or attach to a tree. They do well in pots. Bromeliads vary as to when they flower. I fertilize mine with a regular landscape fertilizer in March, June and October. A bloom special type fertilizer would encourage quicker flowering. They flower when they are ready to, so forcing the issue is only marginally effective.

Q. Will a large **staghorn fern** that completely encircles the main stems of my grapefruit tree hurt the tree?
A. The fern just uses the tree for support; it will not harm it in any

way. If the fern were located on a smaller branch, the fern's weight could break a branch.

Q. My **staghorn fern** is growing on a board that has gotten too small. **How do I separate it** and make new boards?
A. You will have to break up the plant to get it off the small board. A sterile knife is essential when propagating to minimize disease problems. Use broken off pups to start new plants. Locate the new plants in an area with filtered sun and fertilize monthly with a weak solution of Peters 20-20-20 from March to October. Why not attach the staghorn directly to a large tree with rough bark like an oak? It can grow naturally there without worry about upgrading board sizes in the future. I have young staghorn ferns on my trees and I do not do anything to them except water them if they are dry. They get nourishment from the decaying leaves collecting around them. Old banana peels are also a food source. Fern baskets can be packed with various products such as shredded tree fern stems or sphagnum moss.

BULLBS

Q. What kind of bulbs can I plant in South Florida?
A. Most bulbs have a fairly short blooming season here. I have tried several kinds with varying success. Eucharis lily is one beauty that is fragrant and likes shade. It has white daffodil-like flowers in February and March. It is very slow growing and somewhat expensive, but I would rate it highly. Rain lily is a small summer bloomer that comes in pink, white or yellow. It is very pretty and is somewhat like crocus. Amaryllis of various colors are available, but the orange-red form is most common here. It blooms in April and all have evergreen foliage. Spider lily is a fragrant white summer bloomer reaching 2-3 feet. Spider lily likes sun. I would try established nurseries for some of these bulbs. Mail order companies like Parks in Greenwood, SC will also carry them.
Q. Can I plant **tulips** here?
A. Tulips are one of those beautiful northern things that take some work to pull off here. They are not suitable in the ground or pots

except for one blooming period. You may be able to purchase them from one of the bulb houses, pre-chilled and ready for planting in the fall. December is the best month to plant tulips. They should be planted about six inches deep and six to seven inches apart. If you are going to chill them yourself, allow 50 to 60 days at 40 degrees in the refrigerator to meet the dormancy requirements. They need full sun to part shade for best results. An eastern exposure may prolong the bloom display. If you are going to use them indoors use an African violet type soil that has good drainage.

Q. We have **amaryllis** bulbs that are multiplying but no blooms. What do you recommend?
A. Amaryllis need full sun and a somewhat dry location for best results. Bulbs should not be planted deeply or they will not bloom. They usually flower in April/May. Have the top of the bulbs just below the soil surface. Lift the bulbs if they are too deep. Fertilize with a low nitrogen fertilizer like 4-6-8 in October and again in March to stimulate growth. If the bulbs were small when moved, they will need several years to attain blooming size. After blooming leave all the foliage on the plant.

Q. We used to dig up our **cannas** and store them over the winter when we lived up north. My cannas bloom all year here, but the foliage looks burned up. What care do they require in south Florida? Sometimes caterpillars that roll up the leaves affect them. Is this a butterfly caterpillar?
A. Cannas can be left in the ground year-round here. They can be divided, as they multiply quickly. They do well at the edge of a pond or canal. **Cannas are best planted at a distance** from your viewing point because the nocturnal canna leaf-roller caterpillar seems to be standard equipment. They chew the leaves and make the foliage look bad but do not affect the blooms. Most leaf-rollers make attractive Brazilian skipper butterflies so just relocate the canna to a less prominent site. The caterpillars can be controlled with Thuricide, an organic caterpillar control. Repeat treatment in 10 days.

Q. Can I grow **agapanthus**?
A. Agapanthus, Lily of the Nile, can be grown here in a sunny,

well-drained location. However, they do not bloom as prolifically as in California. The heat and humidity may be the problem.

Q. Could you tell me who sells **oxalis bulbs**? I would like the green-leafed version.
A. The green-leafed version is a weed in many lawns. Some nurseries sell the white-flowered version as the shamrock for St. Patrick's Day. It is hard to find locally except around the holiday. Bulbs can be purchased from the catalog of George W. Park Seed.(See supplier's list)

Q. My **crinum lily has red spots**. I used fungicide but the problem still persists. What do you recommend?
A. This is a common problem with Asian crinum lily in South Florida. It has rust, which can be controlled with copper fungicide. It's a persistent problem but does not seem to seriously affect the crinum. Continue spraying or just cut off the bad lower leaves. Water in the morning only to reduce fungal problems.

BUTTERFLY GARDENING

South Florida's climate offers gardeners the opportunity to attract butterflies every month of the year. There are **about 160 species of butterflies in Florida**. You can make them a part of your garden.

First some facts about our flying friends.

> Butterflies do **not bite or carry disease**. In their adult form they do no harm.

> Butterflies are **cold blooded**; they do not produce metabolic heat like humans, so they must rely on the sun to raise their body temperature so they can move about. Some bask with their wings open, others with wings shut.

> Many butterflies are **territorial** and fight, chasing others out of their territory.

Butterflies **can see ultraviolet light** (light invisible to the human eye) which makes the markings on flowers very vivid to them and guides them to the nectar tubes. Some butterflies have ultraviolet reflectants or markings on their own wings which are visible only to other butterflies.

Butterflies are **pollinators.** While they are not as abundant as bees, they do offer a particularly **valuable contribution to the continuation of genetic diversity**. Unlike bees which tend to be home based, butterflies move randomly over the landscape. We know of certain plants such as the Florida scrub blazing star and Curtis milkweed that seem to be totally dependent on butterflies of pollination (both species are on the endangered species list).

If you want to bring "flying flowers" into your yard, you need to plant nectar plants, that supply food for the butterflies, and larval plants, which are the food source for the caterpillars. Selecting the nectar plants is easy because butterflies and birds will take nectar from a wide variety of flowers. Generally these are plants have sweet smelling flowers in warm colors such as yellow, red, orange and blue blossoms. By selecting plants that have an abundance of nectar, you will have a cloud of butterflies beating their wings to your garden path.

Now, you have a fast food restaurant. However, if you want future generations to be born in your yard, you need to select larval plants for the butterflies to deposit their eggs. Just as you and I have different ethnic food preferences, different species of butterflies show a preference for different species of flowers. Certain species of butterfly choose specific plants as the food source for the cater-pillars and will lay their eggs only on that particular plant.

Quick start menu:

If you have just a small space and you want to get started what plants would you choose?

I'd start with pentas, firebush and lantana interspersed with parsley, dill and fennel. Next, I'd place a vine (passion flower or pipevine) on a fence or topiary frame. You can make a pole frame by tying long bamboo poles together and pushing them in the dirt. Plant a vine at the base and watch it climb!

For more ideas and information:

Visit
Butterfly World at Tradewinds Park South,
3600 West Sample Road, Coconut Creek, Florida

Surf the Internet
Start at the Association for Tropical Lepidoptera at **http://www.troplep.org** They have many links to follow to other web sites that feature butterflies

The Florida Federation of Garden Club pages have monthly tips, photos, and many links **http://www.ffgc.org**

Books
Florida's Fabulous Butterflies by Thomas Emmel
Photography by Brian Kenney World Publications ISBN: 0-911977-15-5

Florida Butterfly Gardening by Marc C. Minno and Maria Minno
University Press of Florida ISBN:0-8130-1665-7

Native Florida Plants by Robert Haehle & Joan Brookwell
Gulf Publishing Company, Book Division, Houston, Texas ISBN:0-88415-425-4

National Audubon Society Pocket Guide, Familiar Butterflies of North America
Alfred A. Knopf, New York ISBN: 0-679-72981-X

Butterfly Gardening for the South by Geyata Ajilvsgi
Taylor Publishing Company, Dallas Texas ISBN: 0-87833-738-5

Larval Plants and the butterflies whose caterpillars feed on them

LARVAL PLANT
Dill, Fennel and Parsley
Ficus (Strangler and Short-leaf fig)
Mallows

Mustard (peppergrass) capers
Nettles, False Nettle
Passion Vine

Pawpaw
Pipevine (Aristolochia)

Red Mangrove
Ruellia
Scarlet Milkweed
Wild Petunia

Wild Lime

Wild Tamarind
Willow

BUTTERFLY
Black Swallowtail
Ruddy Daggerwing
Tropical Checkered
  Skipper, Painted Lady
Great Southern White
Red Admiral
Zebra Longwing, Gulf-
  Fritillary and Julia
Zebra Swallowtail
 Polydamas and
  Pipevine Swallowtail
Mangrove Skipper
Malachite, White Peacock
Monarch, Queen
Buckeye, White Peacock,
  Malachite
Giant Swallowtail, Shaus
  Swallowtail
Large Orange Sulphur
Viceroy, Eastern Tiger
  Swallowtail

Some Nectar Plants you may wish to include in your garden:

Ageratum – For Monarchs, Queens and Blues
Blue Porterweed (*Stachytarpheta spp.*)– A favorite of many.
Butterfly Bush (*Buddelia davidii*) – For all butterflies including the larger Swallowtails and Fritillaries
Cosmos – Monarchs
Citrus – Swallowtails
Dune Sunflower (*Helianthus debilis*) – A good ground cover and nectar plant.
Firebush (*Hamelia patens*) – Zebras and Sulphurs adore it!
Geiger (*Cordia spp.*) – Smaller butterflies and hummingbirds love it.
Golden Dewdrop (*Duranta erecti*) – A food source for birds too.
Heliotrope – A very fragrant attractor.
Hibiscus – For hummingbirds and butterflies
Lantana – Another all around butterfly favorite
Liatris – Spikes of dark purple attract many species
Mexican Flame (*Senecio confusus*)- Put it on a wall or trellis
Peregrina also called **Jatropha** (*Jatropha hastata*) – A small tree with red blossoms and lots of butterflies
Pentas – Especially the red, magenta and white
Pink Porterweed – Zebras and Sulphurs
Scarlet Milkweed – Monarchs and Queens
Scarlet Sage (*Salvia coccinea*)– Butterflies and hummingbirds
Wild Coffee (*Psychotria undata*) – Zebras
Zinnia – Black Swallowtails

And the **bedding plants**: aster, bachelor button, daisy, impatiens, marigold, petunia and verbena.

GARDEN VISITORS

Q. We have enjoyed watching **hummingbirds** at my son's feeder in Virginia. What time of year can we expect hummingbirds here and what can we plant to attract them?
A. Hummingbirds usually are seen here in the fall and spring although some stay through the winter. They favor red/orange tubular flowers for feeding. Use firebush, firespike, pentas, necklace pod and firecracker to encourage them to visit.

Q. Can you give me some **information about birdscaping?**
A. Birds need a consistent supply of water, food and a safe nesting place. They prefer native plants because they are well adapted to them. Plant a red cedar grove with marlberry and beautyberry beneath to provide different plant levels, cover, and a good food source. Other bird-attracting trees include oak, red maple, dahoon holly, mulberry and lysiloma among many others. Large shrubs could include golden dewdrop, marlberry, wax myrtle, elderberry and eleagnus. Smaller shrubs could include Surinam cherry, *Viburnum suspensum* and rose. Vines could include Mysore blackberry and Virginia creeper. Your local library, botanical gardens and bookstores have good sections on Florida birds and wildlife. To get your garden certified through the Florida Wildlife Habitat Program, you will need pictures, a landscape plan, a plant list and provisions you have made for food, water and shelter. If you are on the Internet go to the website for the Florida Cooperative Extension Services wildlife page at http://www.wec.ufl.edu/Extension/ where you will find all the information you need.

Q. Something is singing at night in my trees. What kind of creature is it that makes such a racket?
A. The noisemakers are probably **tree frogs**, which are very beneficial amphibians. They kill many mosquitoes, flies, cockroaches and other noxious insects and often hang around outdoor lights where insects congregate. The racket is usually connected

with mating and does not last long – just a few weeks. I would suggest coexistence as the frogs perform such a good service for us year round. There are no chemical controls, as the tree frogs are considered very beneficial.

Q. I have **striped snails** living in my citrus tree. How do I get rid of them?
A. The small striped snails do no harm to the citrus tree. I would leave them alone. They feed on lichens and algae that grow on the bark of citrus and other trees. Some of these snail varieties are found on only one specific island in the Keys. They are very beautiful and should be preserved.

Q. Can you tell me what happened to the small **green chameleons** that we used to have in Florida? Now we have the much larger curly-tailed lizards in their place.
A. The small green chameleons were probably eaten by the larger curly-tailed lizards. The somewhat larger Cuban anole also has displaced the native green anole in Southern Florida.

Q. I am going crazy here with so many **wiggly creatures** crawling around. There are **lizards** all over my screened-in patio and they crawl up into the tubing of my patio furniture. How can I get rid of them?
A. The small lizards that you find in your patio are very beneficial in the yard. They eat palmetto bugs and many other noxious insects and do not harm plants. If you have a screened patio I would check for openings where the lizards could get in. Seal the openings with strip insulation or other filler. I would flush the tubes of your patio furniture with a garden hose. Again, seal the tube ends to prevent the lizards from entering. I do not know of a commercial spray for lizards. Ammonia could be used but would kill plants and grass. I would prune back overgrown shrubbery in the area. The lizards prefer vegetation to hide in.

HEDGES

Q. What can I plant at our condominium that is **colorful and requires little care or water**? I need two plant choices for along the sides of 24 buildings.

A. Between the windows, plant variegated arboricola, a colorful hedge with green and yellow leaves. It will grow in all exposures except deep shade. Space 2-2 ½ feet apart and plant out beyond the drip line of the eaves so they can get natural rainfall. Plant Indian hawthorn under windows in sun or shade. Space 1½ feet apart. Water daily for the first two weeks to get them established and then twice a week if there is no rain.

Q. Our homeowners association wants to plant 2,500 feet of hedge. About 700 feet will be planted under ficus trees about 12 feet from the trees. What hedge do you recommend to be maintained at 4 feet against a 6-foot chain link fence? Is **ficus or eugenia** a better choice? What about planting **arboricola** in the shady area?

A. My first thought is to maintain the hedge at just over 6 feet so you do not see the fence. The eugenia or Surinam cherry hedge will take a lot more shade than ficus, and it doesn't have invasive roots. The cherry takes pruning well and is an excellent hedge for sun or shade. The arboricola is good in shade but does not look good as a clipped formal hedge. Its growth pattern and foliage are too coarse. *Viburnum suspensum* is another possibility; it tolerates shade and stands clipping well.

 Surinam cherry hedge is one of our tougher plants. It can endure heavy shade or full sun quite well. Your plants are small but will grow rapidly once established. Use aged cow manure or Milorganite in the planting hole if you wish. These products will not burn the tender plant roots. You can space the plants as close as 18 inches for a fast effect, although 2-2 ½ feet is more normal spacing. The new plants will grow quite rapidly for you – 2-3 feet a year. Watering will be most critical the first three or more weeks.

Daily watering with a soaker base is essential. Water in the morning only for about half an hour. After three to four weeks, the regular sprinkler system schedule should be fine. Make sure all of the plants are covered by the system before you remove the soaker hose. This plant can be maintained as a hedge from 2 ½ feet to 8 feet in height. Prune the plants after they grow to the desired height to encourage fullness of growth. Ultimately prune the hedge like a flat topped pyramid so the lower branches receive adequate light and you have a full hedge to ground level. This is one of the best foundation plants for hard to maintain condominium grounds Surinam cherry has edible fruit which can be used in jams or jelly.

Q. I live next to a **wetland area** and near a very busy road. What could I use for a **hedge** in such an area that would comply with wetland restrictions?
A. I think native **cocoplum** would make a good hedge. It is tolerant of wet conditions and grows thickly, but does not do well in shade.
Q. What is wrong with my **ixora hedge**? It looks sick and has **black smudges.**

A. You could have several problems. All your plantings need to be fertilized in March, June and October with an ixora/gardenia fertilizer if they all look chlorotic. Poor air circulation, excess watering and watering at the wrong time of day causes fungal conditions. Plants used as hedges have poor air movement because of the dense growth and are prone to fungal problems. Water in the morning only between 2 and 10 a.m. to avoid fungal leaf spotting. You can spray with Daconil, but most of the old leaves will fall off as new growth begins. Sooty mold (the black smudges) on some of your leaf samples indicates sucking insects such as scale or mealy-bugs. Treat the shrubs with a systemic insecticide such as Orthene.

Q. We live inland where it gets **fairly cold.** What can we plant **under our windows? They face the north and are in the shade.**
A. Low plantings for wider windows could include Wheelers pittosporum (in dry location) and Schillings holly. Both plants will grow on a north-facing exposure in shade.

Q. What can we grow as a **flowering hedge** near a fence?
A. 'Nora Grant' ixora blooms well with large pink flowers. It will

reach 6-7 feet in time. It blooms year-round if it isn't pruned. Flowering plants bloom at the ends of the branches so pruning cuts off the flowers.

Q. We live in a town house that has a **30-inch height requirement** for hedges in our front yard. What should we plant?

A. Most shrubs in Florida grow quickly and will exceed the 30-inch height in no time at all. I would recommend low shrubs that stay naturally around 3 feet in height with no trimming necessary. My first choice would be Indian hawthorn, which normally has white flowers six to seven months of the year. A pink flowering form is seen in California and may be available here. Space the plants about 2 feet apart. They are slow growing and should not require any pruning. Shillings holly is another low growing choice for a formal shrub without blooms and very tiny neat foliage. You may want higher plantings for the corners of the town house such as *Viburnum suspensum*, which is amenable to pruning and reaches 5 to 6 feet in height.

Q. What is the **best plant to hide an air conditioner**? I need it to grow at least 3 feet in height …fast!

A. Keep all plantings back from the air conditioner to allow for servicing and air movement. Fishtail fern would be a good choice for a 3 foot tall screening plant for the shade. It would not need pruning and is a relatively trouble-free native. The 3 foot height range is a hard one to reach with some shrubs. Most of the good shrub choices (Indian hawthorn, *Viburnum suspensum*, and Shillings holly) are slow growing. I've seen liriope 'Evergreen Giant' grow 3 feet tall in good condition, so this might be another possibility.

Q. Can you **recommend a thorny shrub** that is not too dense but will keep people from cutting through our property? I was thinking about using pyracantha or crown of thorns. We live in Port St. Lucie.

A. Pyracantha is a tall shrub that grows about three to four feet a year and can reach 15 feet. It is thorny and has small white flowers and red or orange fruit. Pyracantha is normally not too dense. The crown of thorns is a slow grower (6 inches to 1 foot a year). It reaches 5 feet in the standard form and about 2 feet in dwarf forms.

It is cold sensitive and could easily freeze at Port St. Lucie particularly if you are west of I-95. It does fairly well on the coast to Vero Beach. The tall form is leggy and has flowers and tufts of foliage at the branch tips. The dwarf form is denser, but at 2 feet is not very practical because all the flowers occur at the branch tips. If you prune it regularly to make it denser, you cut off all the blooms. Thorns can mean lawsuits if you place these plants too close to sidewalks, roads, etc. where people pass. My own choice for a somewhat thorny hedge for your area is silverthorn (*Elaeagnus pungens*). Spaced about 2 ½ feet apart they grow quickly into a nice tight hedge. In the fall, the plant has small white flowers that are very fragrant. Give it plenty of room. If left alone it can reach 10 feet across and 10 to 12 feet tall. It is naturally dense growing. The fast rate of growth means pruning fairly often. Silverthorn is drought and salt tolerant. Keep grass away from the base of your hedges and trees. I have seen too many plants girdled by the weed trimmer and killed.

Q. We have **two big ficus trees and a ficus hedge** near our swimming pool. The owner has no objection to the trees being pruned. **Will pruning encourage root growth**?

A. A ficus hedge is a ficus tree in waiting. The trees definitely have invasive potential. Pruning may slow down some root growth temporarily. I would recommend you contact Arborist's Supply House in Oakland Park. They carry Deep Root Barrier, which could deflect the roots away from the pool. It is expensive but worth the trouble.

Q. Where can we get more information on **Surinam cherry and orange jessamine** and where can they be purchased?

A. Surinam cherry is a good hedge plant. It is also grown as a small tree and can grow to 15 feet or so. It has foliage similar to ficus but without the bad roots. Orange jessamine also can be used for hedge work or as a small tree. The 'Lakeview' variety has larger flowers and fruit and is a bigger, faster grower. Flowers are very fragrant and small red fruit is decorative. Blooms usually occur near the time of the full moon, which seems typical of many fragrant white flowering plants. Both plants can seed in woodlands so may be a pest in native areas. These shrubs are easily obtainable at most garden centers.

Q. My **orange jasmine hedge** is yellowing and dying off. What can I do to save it?
A. Judging from the foliage, the hedge needs fertilizer. Use an acid 10-5-5 palm fertilizer to help restore growth to the plants. If the plants were planted too deep or growing near cement similar conditions would be apparent.

HERBS

Q. What do you recommend for growing **thyme**? Ours dies off after we plant it.
A. Thyme is a cool weather herb. Plant it in October and expect it to die off about May.

Q. Can **garlic** be grown in Florida?
A. Garlic will grow here, but does best in the cooler months from October to May.

Q. I have two **problems with potted chives and parsley** on my balcony. Tiny oval **black bugs** attack the parsley and then it turns brown and dies. A **white dusty coating** develops on the stems and leaves get variegated and die. I fertilize all my plants with Miracle-Gro and I recycle the soil and bake it in the oven at 225 degrees for one hour. I wash the pots with bleach and clean them. Is this a waste of time?
A. Use fresh sterilized potting soil. The old soil probably contains a lot of soluble salts, which can do a plant in. The salts make unglazed clay pots turn white. This could be the film on your plant stems. Or the film may be **powdery mildew**, a fungal disease. Water your plants only in the morning to avoid fungal problems. Mealy bugs also can give stems and leaves a whitish cast, but they are solid and usually fuzzy. Safer's insecticidal soap should take care of them. The little black insects you mentioned may be **fungus gnats** that feed on roots. Again, a soap drench of the soil should cure that problem. Repeat the soap treatment in seven to ten days to kill hatching eggs.

Q. I have tried growing **basil** inside and outside with poor results. I buy good looking plants, and within a month the **leaves get brown spots or white wiggly lines appear** in them. What can I do for better results?

A. The brown spots mean your basil has **fungal leaf spot**. Water the plant in the morning only and keep the foliage dry. Locate the plant in an open place with good air circulation to minimize fungal problems. Basil is used in cooking, so I do not want to recommend any pesticides. If insects attack the basil, spray with an organic pesticide (some cayenne pepper and two teaspoons of liquid soap to a gallon of water). This should take care of most bothersome insects. The leaves are fine for cooking if you rinse them well before using. Another problem with basil is **leaf miner**. A small worm tunnels inside the leaf and often leaves a wiggly trail on the leaf. Spraying is not practical as the caterpillar is inside the leaves. Grow the plant on a screened porch or windowsill indoors where the leaf miner moth can't reach them to lay eggs. Pick off and throw away all bad leaves. Dispose of any old leaves lying on the potting mix. Sanitation should break the life cycle of the moth and prevent the leaf miner.

Q. I have difficulty growing **lavender** here. Do you have any tips?

A. **Lavender** is a cool-weather plant that is not permanent here. Plant it in October and enjoy it over the winter. It will fade away in April or May when the weather warms up again. It can get **powdery mildew**. Take care to water in the morning only and spray with a fungicide like Daconil.

Q. I grow **basil from seed** and the plant grows only to a foot tall and then wilts and dies. I fertilize once a week with Miracle-Gro and use a potting soil to which I add some cow manure. The plant grows on my screen porch.

A. I would clean the pot out with Clorox and rinse thoroughly. Use new potting soil mixed with 1/3 perlite or vermiculite to promote drainage. I would skip the cow manure.

Q. **What herbs can grow on a screened porch** in pots?

A. Most herbs will grow nicely on a porch as long as they receive sun for 4-5 hours a day. The herb season starts in October and ends about April-May. Some herbs like rosemary can continue from year to year but most die off from the heat and humidity during the summer.

Q. Does **curly parsley** like sun or shade? My plant in the sun does not look good. Should I fertilize it when I water it?
A. I would locate the plant in bright indirect light and fertilize every two weeks with Peters 20-20-20. The plant should last till late spring before it dies off.

HOUSE PLANTS

Some people have no outside area for potted plants so must grow them inside. The inside environment offers many more challenges for good plant health. The low humidity caused by A/C and heat is fine for succulents but causes a real strain for some of the tropical types. The availability of good light can also be a problem. I would stick to the most reliable types for interior use. Be very careful about new plants introduced into the house. Put them in a separate room for a month or so to observe for any plant pests or diseases. You can then include them with your other houseplants if healthy. The worst interior pests include scale, mealybugs and spider mites. The best time to propagate any plant is during the growing season – April-August. Repot most houseplants by the second year to a larger pot because the original soil gets exhausted. Apply the same care for this plant as your other houseplants. Don't overwater, use a liquid fertilizer monthly between March and October and watch for brown tips on the leaves, which may indicate excessive salt buildup. As new leaves develop on stem tips, the oldest ones die off. The plant can support only a certain number of leaves depending on its health and vigor. If the newer leaves closer to the end of the stems are in trouble then you have a problem. Consider flushing the soil with water to leach out excess salt and repot every two years

Q. My **variegated ivy** has scale and I have tried to kill it with warm water. I have Schultz Instant insect spray. Should I try this on the ivy? Should I propagate it?

A. Ivy is hard to grow here. Dexol Systemic Houseplant granules should control the scale. I would propagate only a clean part of the plant. Isolate the ivy from your other houseplants. Spider mites can also attack ivy. If they appear, take your plant outside in a shady location such as a screen porch and hose it down with a strong jet of water to wash away the mites.

Q. Can you tell me what is attacking my **Swedish ivy and gardenia**?

Q. My **pothos** has some **yellow leaves** but most of the plant continues to look good. Is this a seasonal event?

Q. The leaves from my **spider plant** fall off every six months or so. Why?

Q. What can I do to stop my peace lily (spathiphyllum) from browning?

A. **The answer to all four questions is the same**. No leaves are permanent and the lower leaves of all plants will drop off as new ones grow. In Florida, leaf drop occurs in the spring, but some leaves may drop at any time. If the top leaves are browning, the plant could be getting too much sunlight. Brown tips on the leaves can be a signal that you are overwatering or have soluble salt problems.

Q. Could you explain why my **African violet** leaves have brown edges? I love the plants and want them to be healthy again.

A. African violets can be a bit fussy. Keep water off the leaves. Salt buildup from long-term fertilizer use can cause brown edges on the leaves. Lower leaves resting on the edge of the pot also will often have brown edges. You may flush the salt from the soil by watering carefully from the top, keeping water off the leaves. Pour water, three times the volume of the pot, through the soil and let it drain out thoroughly. For example, if you had a 1-gallon pot, pour 3 gallons of water through the soil to flush away the salt buildup. Sometimes cyclamen mites can be a problem indoors, but they are microscopic and hard to see.

Q. My **African violets** do not bloom. They get strong indirect light and I feed the plant with violet food. Would they be better in a clay pot? How do I propagate them?

A. African violets should be placed a few feet from a window but not in direct sunlight. A 15-30-15 liquid fertilizer applied monthly or fish emulsion every second month will help blooming. A well-drained plastic pot is preferable to a clay pot. Water can be applied when the top layer of soil feels dry. Keep water off the leaves. A dish with stones and water below the stones will help to keep humidity up around the plant. Propagation is time consuming but effective. Take a leaf from the oldest outside ring of foliage and cut it off as close to the main stem as possible. Recut the stalk to 2 inches in length. A rooting hormone on the base of the leaf will hasten rooting. Fill a clear plastic shoe or sweater storage box half full with vermiculite and add enough water to moisten the vermiculite. Insert the stems in the vermiculite but do not have the leaves touch it. Punch some holes in the lid and put the container in bright indirect light. Once roots have formed on the stem it can be transplanted to a small pot and grown on as a regular plant. Small leaves should soon appear and will continue to grow with good care.

Q. My **Chinese evergreen** is growing well, but the flowers turn yellow and die before they open. What is wrong?

A. Chinese evergreens have small flowers similar to peace lily. They are not considered important. The foliage with its pretty patterns and colors is the main feature of these plants.

Q. What is wrong with my **jade plant**? The leaves are rotting and have a black crust on them.

A. Your jade plant has been overwatered and may not be salvageable. Try to propagate new cuttings if it still has healthy branches. Plant in an unglazed clay pot using well-drained African violet or cactus soil mix. They should root well and establish in about two months or less. You could try to repot the old plant if is not too far gone. Jade plant does not grow much during the shorter days of winter. Wiping the leaves with alcohol will help control possible mealybug or scale. Jade plants will flower after many years. The plant has white-star like blooms during the spring and summer in drier climates like Southern California.

Q. Do **dracaena and ti plants** make good houseplants?

A. Dracaenas – corn plants and the marginata types – are generally fairly easy to take care of. Their care is similar to dieffenbachia. They are very subject to root rot and can not tolerate excessive water. A clay pot is best for dracaena culture. Avoid scale by using a systemic houseplant insecticide for control. These plants would do better on an outside porch or in the ground if you want to avoid the extra work involved. Both dracaenas can reach 15 feet in height in the ground so place then where there is sufficient vertical room for proper development.

Q. My **corn plant**, which is planted near a staircase, has brown leaves on the edges. I cut off the brown leaf edges every few weeks.
A. Replant your corn plant away from the staircase where it can grow to its proper size. Use it outdoors under trees or along a fence line. Corn plants like some shade. In its old location, substitute the **dwarf *Dracaena thalioides***, which grows only to 3 feet and tolerates dark conditions better. Old bottom leaves will drop as new growth starts, so expect some brown leaves. All plants have them now and then.

Q. How can I get my potted **amaryllis** to bloom again?
A. Do not try to force amaryllis; the bulbs get exhausted and results are spotty. We are fortunate in that amaryllis will bloom and grow naturally outside with little care. Plant in a sunny, well-drained area with the top quarter of the bulb above ground. Do not cut off any leaves; they are next year's energy source for blooms. Expect flowers in April-May.

Q. Can I prune a tall **dieffenbachia** in a large pot?
A. Cut your dieffenbachia off at any height just above a leaf and replant the top in another pot. Remove the lower leaves before you insert the top in the soil. The original plant will resprout and may develop several stems where it was cut. Dieffenbachia is a good interior plant that eventually can reach 5 feet or more in height. It is a leggy grower. It loses old leaves on the bottom and adds new leaves on the top. As long as the top and bottom leaves stay in balance (a bottom leaf is lost – a top leaf replaces it), then I would not worry about the plant. Keep dieffenbachia on the dry side. Water it thoroughly until water comes out the bottom of the pot then

let it alone until the soil is dry to the touch, then water again. Dieffenbachia likes strong indirect light in a west or south window in front of a sheer curtain.

Q. My planter is in a **dark area**. I don't want to use a spotlight on it. What can I grow there?
A. You can try snake plant, either the tall green or variegated forms, or the dwarf Hahn's sansevieria. The old-fashioned Victorian favorite, cast iron plant, may also work. If these don't work, try silk plants.

Q. Are there any houseplants that **produce flowers**?
A. Corn plants, other members of the dracaena group and snake plant produce fragrant flowers after a long period of time. All foliage plants produce flowers, but most of them are not particularly noticeable.

Q. Why is my **ficus dropping leaves** all over the place?
A. Ficus trees often drop leaves excessively in interior situations. They are very sensitive to changes in humidity and light. Locating the tree by your patio door is good, as ficus needs a lot of light for good growth. I suspect low humidity levels in your dwelling with the air conditioner on. Ficus often drop leaves when humidity is lowered. Try locating your tree outside on your patio where humidity will be high and you can still enjoy your tree. It will do much better in an outside environment.

Q. Can I bring my **aralia** indoors?
A. Ming aralias can be grown as a houseplant but are quite temperamental about watering schedules and very subject to spider mites. Ming aralias like humidity, but want to be kept on the dry side. Air conditioning is also a strain on the plant. I would plant it outside and enjoy it. Locate the plant so it gets morning sun if possible. If you leave it in the pot, make sure that it doesn't dry out excessively.

Q. My **fern** fronds are turning brown and dropping off. I think they are dying. How can I save them?
A. Ferns are difficult indoors, as they need high humidity and good

watering to do well. A bright bathroom or kitchen are the best choices for those conditions inside. Better yet, if you have a shady balcony or screened porch, the fern should do well. Some ferns develop their fruiting bodies (spore cases) at the ends of the leaves on the undersides, which may give a brown cast to the plant. Spider mites, scales, whiteflys or other sucking insects could be attacking the foliage. Ferns are extremely sensitive to pesticides and burn easily. Safer's Insecticidal Soap controls many of the sucking insects that bother ferns. If the fern is in a pot, you could dip the foliage in a soapy solution at the kitchen sink. Use Ivory liquid soap, about 2 teaspoons per gallon of water, and turn the fern upside-down, holding the rootball in the pot. Dip the top of the fern in the soapy water to the rootball several times for good coverage. Let the fern sit for five minutes or so and then rinse it off. You also can prune off affected fronds.

Q. What is causing my **hoya to have a sticky residue**?
A. Your hoya probably has a sucking insect such as scale or mealybug feeding on it. Dexol's systemic houseplant granules will control the insects.

Q. **My interior palms are getting spots on the leaves and brown tips**. What is it and how can it be prevented?
A. Palms can be a little difficult in interior settings. The brown spots are fungal leaf spots. Try to water in the mornings so the leaves can dry off during the day. Night watering can promote spotting. Foliage should be rinsed off periodically to minimize dust buildup and insects. Brown tips usually indicate a salt buildup in the plant's pot.

LAWNS

Q. I have a number of **weeds in my lawn and between my patio stones**. I used a week-and-feed product and almost burnt up my lawn. What do you advise?
A. Reduce your irrigation schedule and raise the mower height to the highest setting. The reduced watering and higher mower setting will make the environment hostile to weeds. Your grass tells you when to water. If the leaves are flat, the grass does not need water. If the leaves assume a sharp "V" shape, they are in slight wilt and need water. If they roll up like a cigar, they are in severe wilt and need immediate attention. Use Roundup or Finale to kill weeds between your stepping stones. Follow label directions and do not apply on a windy day because these products kill anything green they touch. It's best to hire a professional service for weed killing. You can wipe the place out with chemicals that are applied incorrectly. Or do like I do. I don't fertilize my lawn because then I have to mow it more. If the grass is mowed regularly, the weeds blend in for the most part.

Q. Is **Zoysia grass** tough against children and dogs?
A. Zoysia is a tough turf. It tends to make a lumpy-looking lawn with a fine texture.

Q. I have a great deal of trouble with my **St. Augustine** grass over the years. A neighbor has a good lawn of **Bahia grass** that seems trouble free. Do you have any comments?
A. Bahia is more drought tolerant and doesn't like a lot of water. It does well in sun and has a finer texture that St. Augustine grass. But it does have some problems. It does not make as thick a turf as St. Augustine does, and it has poor shade tolerance, so use groundcovers in shady areas. Also, it tends to attract mole crickets.

Q. My **St. Augustine lawn has lost its deep green color** although I fertilize in March, June and October with Lesco products. There seems to be a pocket of air between the runners and the turf. The grass is spongy to walk on. What do you recommend?

A. Your lawn may need to be verticut to rejuvenate it. Some companies can perform this service where the runners are vertically cut and the lawn is improved. The lawn will look somewhat torn up after verticutting and take time to settle back in. Years ago some companies would sand lawns, filling in low areas with sand to remove air pockets. This process was best done in summer as the grass was growing more rapidly and would recover more quickly. Disease was commonly a problem with the sanding technique. Both techniques have some disadvantages but should be explored.

Q. I heard that it is necessary to **"top dress"** your lawn here. What is that and how do you do it? Also what about **rolling?**

A. Top dressing lawns was popular some years ago, but is not a common practice now. The practice can increase fungal problems and introduce weed seeds. Sterilized soil is expensive. Sand is often used in top dressing, as it is relatively sterile. I would top dress only sunken, depressed areas of the lawn. The best time is early summer, June or July, when the grass is growing quickly and can recover fast from the treatment. Lawn rolling is more a northern procedure in lawn care. You seldom see it done here except on golf courses.

Q. Can I plant **rye grass**?

A. Rye grass seed is generally a waste of time as it is temporary. Bahia is the main grass grown from seed in south Florida. June or July are good months to establish Bahia. St. Augustine is the other popular type grass for south Florida. It is normally sodded or plugged into the desired area. Do not throw away money trying to grow grass in moderate to heavy shade. Grass is a sun lover and will thin out and die under shade conditions.

Q. What can I do about **sandspurs**?

A. Granular weed and feed products containing asulam will eliminate sandspurs, but need to be used with a great deal of caution. Weed and feed products have burned up many lawns and can kill trees and shrubs if over-applied, and not reading the label can cost you an entire landscape. The product cannot be applied if the temperature is over 85 degrees. The best months for application are from mid-February to early April or late October to early December. You might try spot treatments with Roundup or Kleenup but their use requires extreme caution. See the next question.

Q. How can I get rid of **nutsedge?**
A. Nutsedge is extremely hard to get rid of. The best current control is to use Roundup or Kleenup to try to kill it. These herbicides are systemic and kill the root system. They do not poison the soil as some other products can. They must be used with great caution, as everything green they touch will be killed. You may have to redo a section of your lawn after using these products unless you have excellent aim. The best time to use them is in the early morning or late afternoon when the wind is relatively calm to avoid spray drifting onto desirable plants. Allow two to three weeks for the weeds to brown out and die. Nutsedge is very persistent so you may have to re-spray if it re-sprouts. Wait until it definitely is dead before re-sodding. Definitely follow label directions exactly.

Q. **I have a lot of shade in my yard**. Can I plant 'Floratam' grass?
A. 'Seville' or 'Bitter Blue' St. Augustine grass is much more shade tolerant than 'Floratam'.

Q. We have a lawn with a crabgrass type lawn. **We have lots of shade** and the grass grows poorly and looks like straw. What grass should I replace it with
A. No grass will grow in complete shade. Your grass is the St. Augustine type. Mulch the areas you want to walk on and invest in a ground cover like sword fern that will cover bare soil areas and eliminate the barren look. Space ferns about 1 foot apart in a staggered pattern for good coverage.

Q. I was away from my home for 18 months and the weeds have taken over. The worst is **puncture vine**. What do you recommend I do for control?
A. Puncture vine would be a good groundcover if it didn't have spiny seedheads. It has bright yellow buttercup-like flowers and will even grow at the beach. Use Roundup herbicide and spray affected areas. Spray before 10 a.m. and make sure the spray does

not drift. After spraying, let Roundup work for about three weeks to kill the weeds. Then plant new sod. Palmetto is the best new St. Augustine variety that does not need much watering or mowing. It is also resistant to chinch bugs.

Q. My lawn has a patch of **mushrooms** in it. What can I do to get rid of them?

A. Mushrooms in a lawn are common in the wet season. They are symptomatic of a decaying root system below ground. There probably was a tree in the area that was cut down and a fungus is returning the root system to an organic state, which is perfectly normal. The mushrooms are above-ground fruiting bodies of the fungus. You can spray copper fungicide, which will offer some control.

Q. What is **the best way to eliminate dollarweed?**

A. **Dollarweed indicates excess watering**. Water no more than twice a week, only in the morning. Put some pans on the lawn to see how much water your heads are putting out. One inch per week should be sufficient. Keep the mower at its highest setting so that the grass will shade out weeds.

GROUNDCOVERS

Ground covers are useful landscape additions that can be used where grass does not thrive. They are very useful to unify a landscape design featuring diverse plantings. They can capture and hide blowing leaves and fruits that would otherwise create a litter problem. Some of the larger ferns like the fishtail and 'Macho' are particularly effect in covering the roots of aggressive trees like ficus, schefflera, bischofia, beautyleaf and others. Groundcovers need less maintenance than lawns and offer an excellent alternative for more mature gardeners who are beyond lawn mowing.

Q. Is there **a groundcover other than grass that can be walked on?**

A. Most groundcovers will not tolerate foot traffic. Dichondra and lippia are shade tolerant, but are considered weeds in most yards. **Wedelia** can tolerate some light foot traffic. It will grow in the sun or shade and can be mowed back (mower set at the highest setting) if it grows too tall. It is very invasive and will climb up into branching shrubs, eventually covering them. I suggest using railroad ties to edge where you want the wedelia to grow. Separate your shrubs and walking areas from the wedelia. If it tries to climb over the railroad ties, trimming it back will be an easy task. Mulch is another possibility.

Q. What can I use for a **narrow garden bed between the house foundation and a walkway** facing north?

A. You could try some of the hardy forms of aglaonema, spathiphyllum, bromeliads, *Dracena thalioides*, Boston fern, spider plants or *Liriope muscari*, which does not get as tall as liriope 'Evergreen Giant'. Make sure you have a watering system or hand water the plants, because anything under eaves will not receive natural rainfall. Insects such as mites flourish under eaves, because the rainfall does not wash them off. If the house needs tenting for termites, all plants behind the tent will be gassed and will die. Decorative stone like red lava rock may be another option.

Q. I'd like a northern looking **groundcover like ivy**. Can I use ivy here?

A. Most groundcovers here do not have a northern look such as ivy. Some ivies have been used outside with some success. The green small-leafed types are best, but will not be as vigorous as in more northern locations. We are somewhat beyond the southern limit where ivy is happiest. Liriope grows north to at least Baltimore and has a grassy look with purple flower spikes. *Peperomia crassifolia* is good groundcover for shade and some people think that it has a northern look. Some groundcover junipers grow here but need full sun to do well.

MAINTENANCE

There is so much to learn about living in south Florida. Our unique wildlife and plants are irreplaceable assets. Our water supply is in jeopardy due to careless dumping and excessive growth and water use. I believe we have a man-over-nature philosophy at work here: Dominate and crush whatever natural is in the way as opposed to using what is present as an asset.

Concerned architects can design housing on pilings with wooden walkways in the old Florida cracker style that complements the environment and does not intrude on it. They are doing this in southeast Florida and in the Stuart area now. The alternative is acres of concrete and high rises.

Tree pruning takes the same man-over-nature form. If the tree or shrub is not pruned into a recognizable geometric shape like a square, circle, triangle, or rectangle then the concrete lovers go mad until the plant is shaped as they want it. The irony of all this is the cost in dollars, unnecessary work year after year, and harm to the plant.

Q. Our tree trimmer **trims the palms using tree spikes**. The spikes put holes in the tree. Will this hurt the palms?
A. Spikes will harm the palms because they cannot heal wounds. The wounds provide openings for disease, termites and carpenter ants. Different palms vary in how quickly they will be affected by the damage. I would get another tree service.

Q. **I always thought trees and shrubs should be pruned after blooming in the fall**.
A. Gardening rules are a bit different in Florida. Up North, where plants might bloom for one to two weeks, it's common to prune them back after they bloom so next year's display is not disturbed. But here many plants bloom year-round, so they can be pruned as needed. **I usually prefer pruning in June or July** because there usually is cloud cover and possible scalding from the sun can be avoided. Flowering plants should never be used for hedges or

foundation plantings that regularly get pruned. All the flowers get cut off and all you have left is a green bush. It is better to use Surinam cherry or *Viburnum suspensum* for hedges. Keep the flowering plants out in open lawn area beds where they can grow freely and not be pruned.

Q. What is the best method of pruning a tree and can you recommend a good tree trimmer?
A. **Pruning** on all plants can be done at any time of year in Florida. In my opinion the optimum season is at the beginning of June through August, before the main hurricane season. Do not allow any hat rackers on your property. These people stub trees back so they look like a collection of sticks. Don't hire someone who appears at your door just because he has a chain saw in his hand. Proper pruning involves cuts made almost flush with stems. Dead wood and crossing and rubbing branches are removed from the interior of the tree. When a tree is properly pruned it shouldn't even look like it has been touched. Go for drop crotch pruning. This is more expensive, but trees do not need pruning more than every five to six years, which will be a big saving. Reputable tree companies practicing the drop crotch method may be hard to find. Make sure they follow the International Arboricultural pruning standards to insure the best care for your trees. Good companies will probably be members of the International Society of Arboriculture, the National Arborist Association or some other professional association. Check Better Business Bureau recommendations.

Q. Our community landscaper just cut my 3 ½ foot tall ixoras full of bloom back to 1 foot. I feel this was the wrong time to cut them back. Can you comment on this?
A. Cutting ixora back to 1 foot in height is radical pruning and hard on the plant. **Never remove more than one-third of the total green growth at one time**. I normally recommend summer pruning as we usually have cloud cover. This protects the plant from sunscald and the plants recover quicker because summer is the major growing season.

Q. How long before we can remove the ropes and stakes from a newly planted tree? Can a tree be injured if a rope is looped around the trunk without some protection?

A. **Trees should not be staked for more than one year**. Bare rope can girdle the tree. Many new staking arrangements are available including staking straps that do minimal damage. Staking is needed only until the tree is established.

Q. **Why are you so militant about not using weed trimmers?**

A. I have seen and heard of many cases of tree death in the past few years from weedtrimmers. The combination of excess watering and trimmer damage set the trees up for an attack of Armillaria root rot. Wounds at the bases of the trunk can girdle young trees and provide an entry point for the spores of this fungus. This aggressive root rot causes rapid decline and death in trees once it is established. There is no control but to avoid mechanical damage and to cut back on watering. Protect the base of the trees with a permanent groundcover planting. Water no more than twice a week in winter and only if needed in the summer.

Q. **Should I use a spreader sticker** with my fungicide for better control?

A. Spreader sticker is a good product to use in conjunction with insecticides or fungicides. It helps the pesticide to adhere better, increasing the effectiveness of the product. Brand names include Biofilm and Lesco Spreader Sticker.

Q. You said in one of your columns that you did not know of **a cleaning product that would clean mildew off shingle roofs without hurting the plants.** I found a good product that works and did not damage my plants. It is called M-1 Deck and Roof Cleaner and is sold as a liquid concentrate in 1-gallon bottles. For roof cleaning I diluted it 7:1. I sprayed it on the roof with a pump type bug sprayer, let it sit for 10 minutes and washed it off with a low-pressure (1,200 psi) pressure washer. A year later my shingles still look clean, and no plants died. The label says it is biodegradable and non-poisonous. The cleaner is made by Jomaps, Inc. in Alpharetta, GA, and is available through Allied Building Products in Fort Lauderdale.

Q. I opened some **2-year-old Miracle-Gro packages**. The product is moist. Is it safe to use?

A. Use it quickly. Most of these products have a short shelf life.

Q. **How close should I place the mulch next to my trees and plants**?
A. Mulch should always be kept way from the bark of trees and shrubs. The mulch keeps the bark wet and prevents it from breathing. This causes the bark to rot and peel off and eventually can kill the tree or shrub.

Q. **Where can I get melaleuca mulch**? Can I use it in all garden areas?
A. Melaleuca mulch is produced in Florida. The company, Forestry Resources, Inc., is located in Ft. Myers. It is utilizing the invasive melaleuca as a mulch product and planting bald cypress in its place. Cutting down cypress trees just for mulch strikes me as very wasteful as cypress wood is very valuable. Mclalcuca mulch should last as long as cypress because the tree is durable and the wood doesn't rot easily. More landscape architects are now specifying melaleuca mulch on their projects. There have been some reports of melaleuca seed sprouting in the mulch, but this is probably on very wet sites. Sprouting is not a problem in eastern areas of Broward and Palm Beach counties where the soil is sandy and dries fast. Melaleuca normally does not germinate in dry areas.

Q. **How do we keep a tree trunk from re-sprouting** after its been cut down?
A. The best way is to have the stump and heart of the root system ground with a stump grinder. Certain vigorous trees resist even this treatment including bischofia, women's tongue and rough lemon. An alternative is to use a herbicide like Roundup or Kleenup on the emerging foliage from the stump and roots. Several treatments may be necessary to kill the tree, particularly if it was large.

Q. What is the **procedure for gathering seeds for propagation**?
A. These steps will work for most any seed.
- Mark the plants you wish to keep for seed. Look for good qualities such as good health.
- Plant only one variety or strain. If you are using other varieties, keep them at least 100 feet apart to avoid cross-pollination.
- Let seed ripen on the plant as long as possible before collecting it. Seed capsules usually are brown when ripe. The pods will

be brittle and should split easily.

- Clean the seed by rubbing it against pieces of wire screening. Various sizes of mesh should be saved for different seed sizes. Seed and chaff will separate by the rubbing process.
- Store seed in a cool, dry place in a covered airtight container.
- Test for germination by placing about 30 seeds on blotting paper or raw cotton in a shallow dish. Keep the paper or cotton moist to hasten germination, but do not let the seed remain in water. Keep the seeds warm and dark. When they germinate note how long it took and the percentage of viable seed that you have. If the seed is moldy it is no good.

Q. I want to **take cuttings and root them**. How do I do it?.
A. **Most cuttings from plants can be rooted in the following manner.** Cut a 5 to 6- inch shoot at a 45-degree angle. Remove the lower leaves. Dip the cutting in Root- tone and plant in a pot filled with a well draining potting soil. Place outside under a tree in the shade, and the cutting should root in a few months. Let it grow to some size before planting it in a permanent location.
Another way to root plants is to try layering the plant. Take a lower branch and scrape the bark off the underside of the branch where it can touch the ground. Put a Root tone hormone on the wound area. Then put soil over the wounded branch area and hold it down with a brick or stone. Make sure the wounded area makes positive contact with the ground. Check in a few months to see if roots have formed. Recover the rooted branch with soil and then after allowing about another six months for root growth, cut it off and replant it if the layering operation is successful.

Q. **What should I do in the garden to get ready for a hurricane**
A. Getting ready for a hurricane is mainly common sense. You probably will be evacuated if you live near the ocean or on one of the barrier islands. I would have a good tree company check my trees and shrubs for problem areas. They should remove branches that overhang your roof. Dead wood and crossing branches should be removed from the tree interior. The tree should be opened up to allow air to pass through. Coconuts should be removed, as they can become bowling balls in a storm. Old fronds can be removed if

they are below the horizontal line on the palm. Upward angled fronds should be allowed to remain. Do not allow tree workers to climb palms with spikes…they can puncture the soft stems of palms like royals and cause rot to occur in the center of the palm stem. Palms cannot heal over puncture wounds like regular trees and shrubs. Put away all potential missiles like lawn furniture, tools, trashcans, etc. Prune shrubbery so it does not rub against the building or screening.

Q. We are having our house tented for termite extermination. Will the gases kill my plants?
A. Yes. The gases can kill houseplants so move these outdoors to a shady place away from the house. Make sure the tent is draped behind the foundation plantings so they are not killed.

Q. Every year we get assessed for tree trimming at our condominium. **Is it a law that trees have to be trimmed each year?**
A. According to Becker and Poliakoff, P.A., a firm specializing in condominium law, there is no state regulation requiring that trees be cut every year in a condominium setting. If trees are properly pruned using the drop crotch method, they can go at least five to six years between pruning jobs. If trees are creating a specific problem such as excessive fruit drop and staining, bad root systems, brittle wood, or other problems, it would be cheaper to remove the tree and replace it with something less invasive and more appropriate to the location.

PERENNIALS

The plants you see at the entrances to condominiums in the winter months are usually annuals such as begonias and impatiens. They make a big splash of color from October to April, but the heat and humidity of summer does them in. If you do not mind the yearly expense, annuals give the best color display of all. Perennials are not as showy as annuals, but last more than one year. Their life span is at least two to three years, and most last longer than that. Low growing perennials (1 to 3 feet) which like full sun include: lantana in yellow, purple, and other colors and bush daisy in yellow and orange. Peace lily in white and justicia in pink or white want shade. Pentas is taller growing (3 to 4 feet) and comes in pink, red, white and hot pink.

Q. Help me save my **pentas**. They are two years old but are dying from the bottom. We did a xeriscape design with our plantings and really love the pentas. Can I start new plants from cuttings?
A. I am very fond of pentas as a fairly tall growing flower that blooms every day of the year. It is a perennial and lasts for a good number of years. Nematodes can attack the roots in sandy soil and stunt growth so it is good to use about 50% peat moss mixed with the existing soil for planting. My pentas have lasted six years and are still doing well. They do not like much water and if they are in an area where water stands or is slow to drain, they will die. They do not like mulch up against the stems because the bark can't breathe. Pull the mulch at least 1 to 2 inches from all plantings. Pentas can be started from cuttings. You will get the best results between April and September.

Q. I planted **ruellia** and after two months they diminished in size. What went wrong?
A. The dwarf ruellia were eaten by snails; use snail bait or diatomaceous earth for control.

Q. I have two **daylily** plants growing only a few feet apart. One blooms and the other has good leaves. They are planted at the same depth. How can I increase blooming?
A. Daylilies need at least six hours of sun to bloom well. They like a well-drained location with no standing water. Fertilize with an acid gardenia/ixora fertilizer to encourage more bloom. Keep mulch away from the plant stems to avoid rot. Most daylilies bloom here in April/May, but there are some new repeat bloomers that can flower on and off until October. Evergreen daylilies do well here, but dormant and semi-dormant varieties do not receive enough of a cold rest period and do not do well. I would hesitate to

order daylilies from mail order catalogues because most varieties they all are semi-dormant or dormant types. Palm Beach Daylily Gardens is a daylily grower who has plants suitable for south Florida.

Q. What can we plant in **a very dry spot** for some color?
A. Try tough, colorful plants such as lantana, pentas, dwarf crown-of- thorns or ruellia. Space about 1 foot apart. If no water is available, wait until June before planting. Then nature will water for you. Add one quarter peat moss to the existing soil to improve its moisture retention. Old shredded leaves, grass clippings, etc., can also be mixed with the existing soil to improve it.

Q. Can you recommend **plants for a wet location** on my center island?
A. Many plants will do well in a damp area. If you want trees, I suggest red maple, sweet bay magnolia, wax myrtle, dahoon holly, red bay, bald cypress, and strawberry guava. Shrubs could include cocoplum, crinum lily, Fakahatchee grass, buttonbush, leather fern, elderberry and Florida privet. Low plants could include lizard's tail, and sword fern.

Q. Can you **recommend some plants for a perennial garden** 4 by 18 feet that faces south? There is some filtered shade from palms.
A. Many perennials last about two years and then die out, as most bloom every day and exhaust themselves. The new tall (3-4 feet) permanent ruellia with blue flowers would be good as a background plant. A midsize pink ruellia is also available. Some of the repeat blooming daylilies would be good additions. You might use dwarf Fakahatchee grass as an accent. Pentas is always good and attracts butterflies in tall varieties to 4 feet and dwarf types, about 18 inches. Their flowers are white, pink, red, purple and lavender. A good ground cover for the front of the bed could be purple fountain salvia. All these plants should last beyond two years.

Q. I ordered **rose mallow** (*Hibiscus moscheutos*) **and rose of Sharon** (*Hibiscus syriacus*) from a catalogue. The rose mallow is blooming beautifully. Will the rose of Sharon amount to anything?
A. Rose mallow is a native in northern Florida. I do not know if it

will be a permanent plant here because we don't have cold periods and the plant needs some dormancy. I prefer to get plants from good local nurseries. Rose of Sharon will grow here, but is out of its best growing range.

Q. Last year you recommended **begonias as a substitute for impatiens** as they were perennials. I purchased **fibrous begonias** which I find are annuals. Can you clarify this for me?
A. Annual begonias have names such as wax, fibrous, semperflorens or bedding begonias which all mean the same thing. They are small mound-like plants used for borders, grow about 1 foot tall and come in red, pink and white. They usually last the entire winter dry season from October to May, can take sun or shade and do not have special excessive watering requirements like impatiens. Perennial begonias come in several classes and are permanent. The **rhizomatous begonias** have creeping roots, showy foliage and white to pink blooms. They flower mostly in winter and spring. The cane type begonias bloom all year on arching canes and can reach 4-6 feet tall. They are troubled by nematodes but are most enjoyable while you have them. Shrub type begonias also bloom most of the year in pink, red, and white. See the Begonia *odorata 'Alba'* discussed under "Plant of the Month" for September.

PESTS AND PESTICIDES

The best advice is to stay away from insecticides unless you see a problem. Pesticides that drip into our waterways cause fish kills and other environmental problems. I recommend that you use organic controls whenever you can. Insects build up resistance to pesticides, creating *superbugs*. Use the safest product possible and make sure you have the problem correctly identified so you will not use the wrong pesticide. Less usually is better than more. I have sprayed only twice on my property in the past 17 years for a localized problem.
General Suggestions
Spray in the early morning or late evening when the temperature is below 85 degrees. Spraying when temperatures are over 85 degrees

can burn leaves and cause leaf yellowing or leaf drop. Do not spray if it is windy as some sprays stain or could hurt adjacent plantings. Copper fungicide is an example as it can stain everything electric blue like your house or paving. Repeat treatment in 7-10 days to kill new pests hatching from eggs. Use a spreader sticker or a few drops of soap with your pesticide mix to help the spray adhere to the plant.

Clearly **many of the most frequently asked questions regarding insects revolve around tomatoes**, those succulent orbs of earthy delight. As versatile as they are delicious, they can be grown in pots on a patio or planted in the yard. One bite will convince you that, whatever their problems, they are worth the effort. From letters and samples sent or presented to me at plant clinics, I present the condensed guide to growing tomatoes.

 They can drive you buggy!

A woman has a small Baggie in her hand. Inside is a branch from a tomato plant. The leaves are green but oddly puckered.
"What's wrong with my tomatoes?" she asks plaintively. The answer is aphids – small, soft-bodied insects that suck plant juices. The telltale sign is the twisted leaves. The remedy is a thorough spray with the garden hose or an application of insecticidal soap.

The next person carries the patient, or a small piece of it, in a plastic dish. Again, it's a tomato plant. **Yellow leaves, with small dark splotches**. Hmmm. Could be blight or maybe leaf spot. Both are treatable, if not curable, with a copper sulfate spray or a weak solution of hydrogen peroxide.

But it could also be fusarium or verticillium wilt, in which case the prognosis is poor. The gardener should have used a disease –resistant variety.

You have to face it. Pests are the order of the day with tomatoes. Expect leaf damage, but don't let it drive you crazy. Some insects, such as leafminer, will make the leaves look awful, but they will not affect fruit yields.

One of the reasons we grow our own food is to have some control over what chemicals go on it. It's best to avoid heavy doses of pesticides. Use commercial insecticidal sprays as a last resort.

Beneficial insects are a good first line of defense. Ladybugs
control aphids, mealybug, scale and other sucking insects. Praying
mantis control larger insects such as grasshoppers, beetles and other
chewing pests. Parasitic wasps lay eggs on caterpillars, such as
tomato hornworm and other larvae. Give the good guys a few days to
start working on the bad guys before you panic. Now, let's get more
specific.

Aphids

Aphids come in many colors, from rosy pink to gray to pale
green and they attack almost anything. Some have wings; others
don't. If your plant is growing slowly, or if the leaves (especially
the tender young ones) look twisted or puckery, check the underside
for these little sap-sucking insects. Their sucking causes distorted
foliage and poor growth. They may also spread tobacco mosaic
virus, a disease fatal to tomatoes.

A strong spray of water will wash them off, but you will
have to repeat the treatment often. You also can use a commercially
prepared insecticidal soap, available at garden centers, to suffocate
them. Or put a couple of tablespoons of hydrogen peroxide in a
gallon of water and spray the plant regularly.

The good news? Aphids are a favorite food for ladybugs.

Stinkbug

An occasional problem on tomatoes and citrus, stinkbug is
a shield-shaped bug about a half inch long. It can be green, black
or brown and can leave a foul odor on your hands if it is handled.

Stinkbug punctures the fruit and sucks out the juices. The
fruit will change color where the stinkbug feeds and leaves a toxin
behind; a tomato will turn white or yellow in the affected areas.

The best control is to remove weedy areas where they hide
close to the tomatoes. If you continue to have problems, dust the
fruit with diatomaceous earth or spray with insecticidal soap.

Cutworm

Cutworm is a major problem for new tomato transplants.
The caterpillar is about 1 to 2 inches long and is usually black or
gray. Active only at night, they hide below the ground during the

day. They chew new transplants off at the ground level and the plant topples over and dies.

The easiest solution is to put a "collar" around the transplant after it is set in the ground. You can use almost any material – cardboard, empty vegetable cans with both ends removed or empty toilet paper tubes. Make sure the collar is pushed down about an inch into the soil and is at least 2 inches high

Tomato fruitworm

Tomato fruitworm is active in south Florida. The caterpillar is about an inch and a half long and can be green, pink or brown. It enters the tomato at the stem end and feeds on the fruit, making it worthless.

Nature can take care of these pests because they are often parasitized by trichiogamma wasps and tachnid flies. Or you can dust the fruit with diatomaceous earth or Dipel.

Tomato hornworm

The tomato hornworm is a big guy – more than 4 inches long- but its dark green color makes it difficult to see in foliage. It gets its name because of a horn at the rear end of its body. One or two of these fellas can eat an entire plant. Leaves may be chewed to the stem; occasionally fruit also will be consumed.

In most cases, they can be picked off by hand and dropped in a can of kerosene or ammonia. The best time to find them is at night using a flashlight, because they hide during the day.

One warning: If you find a hornworm or other caterpillar with small white sacks on its back, leave it alone. The sacks contain the larvae of a small wasp that preys on the hornworm and other caterpillars.

HOW TO COMBAT PESTS

The most annoying part of growing vegetables is coping with pests and diseases. Here are some tips on how to control them:

- If an insect problem is not excessive, picking the pests off the leaves or blasting them with water can be effective.
- Insecticidal soap is useful for sucking insects. Follow label directions and spray on the underside of the leaves before 10 a.m. or in the evening; repeat spray a week later.
- Never spray if pollinating bees or wasps are working the flowers.
- Beneficial nematodes kill many soil-borne insects, including cutworms and beetle and weevil larvae that can chew foliage and roots of many plants, including tomatoes. Spray them in the garden with a hose and water.
- *Bacillus thuringiensis* (also called B.T.) is marketed as Thuricide, Dipel, or Biotrol. It's an organic specific stomach poison for use on caterpillars such as hornworms and fruit-worms. New strains have been developed for grasshoppers and other insects.
- Diatomaceous earth is composed of ground-up fossilized one-celled creatures from prehistoric times. The powder can be sprinkled around the base of plants to stop slugs, snails and other insects from crawling up plants and feeding.

Q. Could you tell me about **grasshopper control?**
A. Look for new grasshoppers to hatch in March or April. They do not fly and can be killed in the early stages with an organic bait product (Grasshopper Attack, Grasshopper Control, Nolo Bait or Semaspore). The bait will also affect upcoming generations. Look for grasshoppers on spider and crinum lily and firebush particularly. An organic control for the very destructive lubber grasshopper is a mixture of hot pepper, soap and water sprayed on the leaves of the affected plants. This mixture will repel the grasshoppers. The big grasshoppers are best killed mechanically, as they become too large to be killed by commercial sprays. The large yellow lubbers do not fly like most of their relatives so are easier to catch and kill. They soon lay eggs and die off.

Q. My pinwheel jasmine and ponytail palms have **black on their trunks and some leaves**.
A. Your plants have **sooty mold caused by sucking insects**. Sucking insects like scale and whitefly create a honeydew secretion. The sooty mold grows on this and causes the blackened leaves.

Organic gardeners can use Safer's Insecticidal Soap, but you must cover all affected areas with the soap, as it is a contact insecticide. You can also use Orthene to control. Retreat in 10 days.

Q. I have potted plants with **ants in the soil**. What can I do to get rid of them before bringing the plants inside?
A. Drench the pot with soapy water to drive the ants out. You may have to repeat the treatment several times.

Q. I have had a bad **snail problem** with my flowering plants. Do you have any organic controls? The bait is not very effective.
A. Many people report success by sinking saucers into the ground and filling them with beer. The snails and slugs drown in the beer; repeat the process until populations are reduced. Another trick is to surround the plants with diatomaceous earth or crushed shells from hard-boiled eggs. The eggshells and diatomaceous earth are sharp and puncture the snails/slugs so they dry out and die. The eggshells will need to be rinsed.

Q. What can do about **black spot** on my roses?
A. Funginex should control black spot. Keep foliage dry. Water in the morning only to minimize fungal problems. The roses should be in an open area, well spaced for maximum air circulation. Rake dead leaves from the ground around the plant to try to break the fungal space cycle. Orthenex is good if you want a combination of insecticide and funcigide.

Q. I have **white fly** on my poinsettia. What can I use to kill them?
A. The sweet potato whitefly has been attacking hibiscus and poinsettia. It is a very stubborn pest. Try a systemic insecticide like Orthene, which makes the whole plant poisonous. You will not have to worry about hitting every leaf as you do with a contact insecticide.

Q. I have a passion vine and hibiscus that produce buds, but the **buds drop off**.
A. You probably have **thrips** which damage new flowers, particularly roses, gardenias and hibiscus. They can be controlled with Orthene.

Q. **Something is putting holes my fruit**. What might it be?
A. The stinkbug often punctures fruit, particularly thin-skinned types of citrus. Small brown scavenger beetles will clean out the interior of the fruit after it has been punctured. Occasionally a fruit rat will eat fruit, but then the hole is much larger in the fruit. Stinkbugs are very mobile, so spraying is not effective. Pick fruit early, just at ripening, to beat this pest.

Q. My **impatiens have deformed curled tips.** They are in pots and in the ground. **I have sprayed Orthene, Di-syston, Cygon, Diazinion, and other sprays and cleaned the pots with alcohol before planting. I have a super strain of whitefly.** My potted hibiscus and mandevilla are affected. **I have used Orthene, Cygon, Thiodan, and Di-syston. The Thiodan and ultrafine oil spray was effective but not for long. The yellow sticky traps worked but filled up very quickly**. What do you suggest?
A. It sounds like you have used everything but the atomic bomb on your plants. Insects can become superbugs with repeated sprays of insecticides as they build up resistance. Your impatiens and mandevilla are high on my **DO NOT** plant list as they have lots of problems. Hibiscus also have problems but usually are more manageable. They are usually big growers to 10 feet plus and resent confinement in a pot for more than two years for the standard landscape varieties. I would plant them in the ground and use something like desert rose as a substitute. If you insist on fiddling around with these troublesome plants you might try a mix of Organocide and Excel which is an organic oil and pyrethrum mix. That should stop the whiteflies. Another option is to choose less troublesome plants for your yard. Wax begonia can substitute for the impatiens and is infinitely less troublesome. A good vine substitute could be Henderson's allamanda.

Q. How can I tell if my plant has **spider mites**? **What do they look like**? How did I get them? Do they fly or crawl and are they going to affect my outside plants? How do nurseries protect themselves?
A. Spider mites are microscopic sucking insects related to the spider. They crawl or can be transported by the wind. Spider mites can be detected if you shake some affected branches over a white

paper. If little eight legged dots are moving around, you probably have spider mites. Verify with a magnifying glass. Heavy infestations sometimes can be detected because the plants have webbing over the needles and branches. Mites are most active in the winter months. They are already outside and since rainfall on the leaves washes them off, they are mainly a winter problem. Nurseries have overhead watering systems, so they don't have a major problem with spider mites. Take your plants outside, under a tree and blast off the mites with a strong jet of water from the hose. Other controls include Safer's Insecticidal Soap or a miticide such as Kelthane. To avoid problems in the dry season, hose your plants off periodically in the morning

Q. We have **a millipede invasion** on our screened porch every fall. What can we do for control?
A. Millipedes live in the grass and normally are not a problem. After a wet summer, they often seek higher ground to avoid overly wet soil. If you water a great deal, like once a day or every two days, you are drowning your plants and inviting millipedes. Get a rain sensor for your irrigation system so it will shut off automatically when it rains. If we have no rain, water no more than two times a week. Remember, interior areas get about 10-15 inches more rain than coastal areas. You may wish to spray a band of Dursban just outside the screened area to form a barrier against the invaders.

Q. What is the best way to get rid of **nematodes**?
A. Nematodes prefer sandy soils. Organic matter such as leaves, peat moss, etc. incorporated into the existing soil will discourage nematodes. Plantings of French marigolds also have a repelling effect if you turn them under the soil after blooming. Consider purchasing nematode-resistant plants to avoid the problem. Some varieties of plants are resistant to nematodes and many woody plants are grafted on resistant wood stock. In you are preparing new ground for planting and want to insure a nematode free area, solar sterilization of the garden plot over the summer is another possibility. Cover the garden tightly with clear plastic for two and a half months from the middle of June to the end of August. The soil will heat up to 130 – 140 degrees, killing nematodes and other pests.

Q. How can I **keep birds off my citrus trees**?
A. The only way to keep birds off your citrus would be to invest in bird netting. Netting is used up north for cherry trees and blueberry plants. Park's Seed and other major mail order houses carry the netting. You might also try hanging a replica of an owl. That seems to discourage many birds. However, you need to move it occasionally or the birds get wise and return when they realize the owl isn't real. I've also seen strips of foil or shiny aluminum pie plates attached to the branches with bits with string, thereby allowing them to flutter in the breeze, used as an avian deterrent.

Q. How do I get rid of **land crabs**?
Land crabs are scavengers and are mainly above ground and active during the warmer months from May through October. They stay in their burrows in cooler weather. These burrows can be 15-20 feet long and reach down to the water table. Moth balls, poisoned bread and sonic systems have little effect on them. No pesticides are currently recommended for their control. They can be caught with crab nets and are edible. People in the Caribbean Islands consider them a delicacy. They keep the crabs captive for two weeks and feed them cornmeal to clean out their systems. It should be possible to control a good part of the local population or at least conjure up a good meal during a crab roundup on one of the full moon nights when they mate.

Q. We just put in pentas around our pool and they disappeared over night, thanks to a **hungry iguana**. What can I do to stop him without killing him?
A. Try using pepper spray, **a homemade mix that will discourage squirrels, rats, birds, insects and iguanas.** Add 2 teaspoons liquid Ivory soap to a spray jar. Put a coffee filter or cheese cloth over the jar mouth and add 2 tablespoons cayenne pepper and 1 tablespoon garlic powder. Add water and let the essence filter into the jar, then spray the foliage. It will not harm the plant or the iguana but it will taste terrible. When it rains the mixture will wash off.

Q. Our condominium is having a rat problem. **Are there plants that attract rats**?
A. A number of plants can attract rats and snakes as they provide good

shelter. Pampas grass harbors these pests and the pandanus or screwpine with its stilt-like roots is also a likely candidate. The screw pine, *Pandanus utilis*, grows in a tree form and is less likely to encourage vermin as it is very open growing. The shrubby clumping pandanus types are more likely to provide shelter as they are very dense. Keep tree and palm branches pruned away from the building, porches, roofs and catwalks to help minimize rat problems.

ORGANIC PEST CONTROL

Organic pest control is the future. Our long history of blitzing property with chemical pesticides has resulted in races of super-bugs immune to most chemical controls. These same chemicals used incorrectly show up in our drinking water and in our food chain. South Florida is extremely vulnerable to this contamination as our drinking water source, the Biscayne Aquifer, runs only 5 -20 feet below ground depending on elevation. Fertilizer dumped on plants, chemical controls over-applied or sprayed when the temperature is over 85 degrees, and herbicides applied during hot weather or excessively lead to dead trees, shrubs, lawns, etc. In some cases with herbicides, the soil is made sterile and nothing can be planted in that location again. Professionals should apply these products, particularly herbicides, to avoid permanent environmental damage and plant loss.

Another factor entering the chemical pest control arena is the Federal Government. Some of the more hazardous chemicals are removed by government regulation. Proper pesticide storage and disposal are also major concerns.

Fortunately, research is being conducted on more organic controls for these problems. Predatory insects and beneficial bacteria can offer excellent control for certain problems. Encouraging birds to the garden is another organic approach. Plant diversity is very helpful. Planting large masses of the same plant encourages pests. Avoid known pest-prone plants in the landscape.

I have a large variety of plants in my yard and have had minimal problems. I sprayed for thornbugs in 1983 and 1984. These pointy pests attack plants in the pea family. Members in my yard that have been troubled include powder puff, tamarinds and some cassias. I did not spray the trees after that and they have been growing fine despite the thornbugs. They may slow the growth somewhat but do not affect the tree severely. I had an outbreak of mealybugs, which aggressively attacked my chenille plant, Turk's cap, and brunfelsia. Wasps and other predators eliminated these pests over a month's time. It is important to realize that most damage is temporary and will not affect plant health in the long run. We must not expect perfect foliage and flowers in outdoor plantings. Nature will usually balance out problems if given enough time.

Plants grown in conditions they like are seldom troubled with pests. Replicate their natural habitat and healthy plants are the result. Do research on the plant before buying it. It is also important to know how big the plant will grow. Give it enough room to develop properly and allow for its mature size. If a mistake is made it will show up quickly on your doorstep. Some south Florida plants can grow 8-10 feet a year because of our long growing season.

Pest-prone plants to avoid or use at the back of the garden include oleander, roses, hibiscus, night blooming jasmine, 'Maui' ixora, canna lilies, red powder puff, angel's trumpet, gardenia and queen palm among others. You can enjoy the flowers from a distance and not see the chewed leaves or other damage. Some of these plants are acid lovers and cannot be used near cement foundations, sidewalks, or patios. They will quickly get chlorotic and die back. Acid lovers include ixora, gardenia, hibiscus, powder puff, orange jessamine, ligustrum, pinwheel jasmine, etc. An acid fertilizer for ixora/gardenia applied in March, June and October will keep them going.

One good overall organic concoction that works well with vegetables and ornamentals is a **soap, garlic powder and cayenne pepper mixture** that can be prepared at home. Add 2 teaspoons of liquid Ivory soap to a gallon jar. Cover the mouth of the jar with a cheesecloth or coffee filter. On top of the filter add 1 teaspoon each of cayenne pepper and garlic powder. Add water to the container through the filter. The essence of the garlic powder and cayenne pepper will go into the jar. This prevents clogging of the sprayer. Remove the filter from the jar's mouth. Shake up the mixture and attach to your sprayer and you are ready to go. The soap smothers sucking insects and the garlic-cayenne mix repels chewing pests.

The only disadvantage is that the mix will wash off in rainy weather and will need reapplication.

Local garden supply stores and nurseries may be a little slow to stock organic products. Many products are unknown locally and others have a specific shelf life. Some may need to be mail-ordered. The more progressive stores will carry products once a demand has been indicated. In the meantime specialty sources will mail order appropriate products to you. One catalog I was very impressed with is The Bug Store. They cover many unfamiliar products. One of the best controls available for lawn and soil pests is the beneficial nematodes. These good microscopic worms have as expiration date, like milk. They are sprayed to control army and sod webworms, chinch bugs, lawn grubs, bad nematodes, and best of all, fleas. Most people spray for fleas and usually do not worry about the other lawn pests. The University of Texas reports 98% flea control with the nematodes. Each treatment lasts about six to eight weeks. The one caution is that the beneficial nematodes are living, so chemical controls should no longer be used, or you kill the good nematodes and defeat the whole principal of organic pest control. This is a life style change as well as bug control.

PLANT CARE IN EMERGENCIES

Sometimes weather conditions arise that can create havoc with our plants. Hurricanes and freezes are the two main weather events that concern us in southern Florida.

Great care is necessary in choosing plants suitable for the environment. Obviously salt-tolerant plants should be used near the ocean and more cold-tolerant types selected for inland locations more subject to freezes. Sometimes we can play with microclimates to some degree. We can locate less salt-tolerant plants on the lee side of buildings where they are protected from salt winds and spray in normal conditions. Tender plants can be located on the south side of buildings where they are protected from cold winds. But extreme conditions with coastal flooding or freezes can eliminate these microclimate plantings.

Hurricanes cause broken trees and branches, salt-water flooding and radical environmental changes for remaining plants.

The first thing to do is wash down plants subject to salt water flooding. Apply as much water as possible. They may survive but it is questionable. Clean up fallen leaves, branches and other debris. This will allow low plantings and lawns to survive. Try to provide shade for potted bromeliads, ferns and other shade lovers by moving them under shrubbery. Sheets may be used to provide cover for other shade lovers in the ground. Fortunately, standing trees will leaf out in a few weeks to provide new shade.

Trees are the biggest investment in the landscape and the ones most likely to be damaged. Palms vary in their wind resistance. Queen palms and coconuts are not that hurricane resistant. The tall veitchia species, royal palms and pygmy date palms are among the most resistant to strong winds. The taller wind resistant palms drop leaves in strong winds and present a bare pole to the strong winds. They develop new crowns after the hurricane passes. It is a good idea to apply copper fungicide to the crown to prevent possible crown rot.

Ideally, standing trees should have broken branches removed by a certified arborist. The arborist will try to balance the tree's crown, remove stubs and crossing limbs and generally open up the tree so air passes easily through. There could be a long wait for a good arborist and you may have to do the work yourself. Shorten broken branches back to an outward facing fork and cut there just above the fork. Large branches may need to be cut at the trunk. Prune just outside the branch collar, which is the raised area on the trunk where the branch meets the trunk. Cut branches on the underside first to avoid rip cuts down the trunk as the limb drops.

Fallen trees are a mixed bag. Rare specimens are worth trying to save. I would be inclined to dispose of the other trees as they have lost 50% or more of their roots and will not be stable again. I have seen trees that were replanted and they fall over again with every strong storm. This applies to palms as well as regular trees. A hurricane does provide an opportunity to plant superior trees to replace the fallen ones. Trees such as sapodilla, live oak, Indian tamarind, gumbo limbo and others have superior wind resistance and should be considered for future planting. Avoid weak sisters like ficus, ear leaf acacia, black olive and bischofia.

Freeze damage is also fatal to many plantings. It is remarkable how cold south Florida's inland sections can get. I remember one cold year where it reached 35 degrees at Fort Lauderdale's airport one mile inland, 27 degrees in Davie about 10 miles inland and 19 degrees at Highway 27 about 20 miles inland. The Gulf Stream has a moderating effect, producing cooler summers and warmer winters along the coast, but the effects do not carry very far inland. The good news is that the cold spells are of relatively short duration seldom lasting more than two to three days.

Try to protect cold sensitive plantings by pulling mulch away from the root systems and watering heavily just before cold weather occurs. The warm soil will release heat and give some protection to smaller plants. Sheets also can offer some protection against freeze/frost damage. Leave cold-damaged foliage in place until March after all danger of freeze has past. This old foliage will offer protection for the plants. The best protection is to avoid planting delicate tropicals in marginal interior areas. Fortunately these cold events may not occur for many years. The Keys are the only truly frost-free place in Florida.

POISONOUS PLANTS

Unfortunately the space available in this book can not do justice to all the poisonous plants in south Florida. I can only treat the subject in a general way, but will give information sources for those who want to do further investigation. Generally most of the poisonous plants cause problems only if they are eaten. Some produce skin irritation if they are touched. Others produce fine pollen that can result in breathing difficulties. The Mounts Horticultural Learning Center has a small area of poisonous plants that can be viewed through a protective fence. (The garden also features many educational classes and use gardens such as groundcover collection, hedge garden, native plant area, salt tolerant plants, tropical fruit and vegetable gardens). The address is 531 North Military Trail, West Palm Beach, Florida. The County Extension offices have literature on poisonous plants. Their phone numbers are in the directory. A good small book entitled *Florida Poisonous Plants, Snakes, and Insects* is available from Lewis Maxwell, 6230 Travis Blvd., Tampa, FL 33610. It is priced around $5, plus shipping. The dean of poisonous plant information was Dr. Julia Morton of the Morton Collection at the University of Miami. Her excellent book, *Plants Poisonous to People in Florida,* is available at many bookstores.

Several web sites offer information on poisonous plants. Two good place to start are:
Medical Herbalism: A Clinical Newsletter for the Herbal Practitioner (a site that contains links to many others) at http://medherb.com/POISON.HTM and Poisonous Plants Guide, Florida Agricultural Information Retrieval System (FAIRS), USA at http://hammock.ifas.ufl.edu/txt/fairs/wg/39633.html The latter is part of the very extensive offerings of plant information from the University of Florida http://edis.ifas.ufl.edu

Q. Is the coral plant poisonous? I have several small plants in my yard.
A. **Coral plant,** *Jatropha multifida*, is a large shrub reaching 15 feet tall. It is very drought tolerant and the flowers are somewhat showy. The plant is a member of the euphorbia family. The seeds are very toxic and the milky sap can cause a rash. Jatropha is very tough and tolerant of abuse. It just requires some sun to survive. I probably would dispose of the small plants unless you want to give one as a gift to someone you don't like.

Q. What is this ferny plant with bright red pea-like flowers that has appeared in my yard?
A. It is **Glorypea rattlebox** (*Daubentonia punicea*). This plant has escaped into the wild in certain areas of Florida. It is poisonous and dangerous for cattle or horses to eat. It is used as an ornamental in California and in parts of Florida. It makes a large shrub or small tree to 15 feet in height. Rattlebox thrives in a sunny, dry area. The flower display is good and quite continuous but I would not recommend planting it and contributing to the invasion.

Q. I grew a **castor plant** from a seed I got in Hawaii. It has grown into a tree with large leaves on top that have fallen off. New small leaves are emerging from the bark. How do I care for it?

A. The castor bean plant is very poisonous and fast-growing. They are weedy and have naturalized in parts of Florida. They like good sun and full drainage. They require virtually no care and can be invasive. I would get rid of it.

PONDS

Q. We have **pseudo-papyrus** around our lake and it is cut down every year. This supposedly keeps it from spreading. Is this cutting necessary? What other shoreline type plants are good?

A. The pseudo-papyrus, also known as umbrella flatsedge, is an aggressive spreader. The spring cutback also eliminates old foliage. Good shore/pond type plants include iris, pickerel weed, duck potato and lizard's tail among others. Fakahatchee grass clumps also make good edge-of-water plantings.

Q. What **floating plants** can I use in my fishpond?

A. You could use a number of floating plants in your pond, particularly if it is in a sunny location. Miniature water lilies, such as 'Margaret Mary', a tropical blue, and 'Dorothy Lamour', a hardy yellow, are excellent for small ponds. Other attractive floating water plants include the yellow blooming water poppy, water lettuce, and water snowflake. Try a few upright flowers at the pond edge such as dwarf papyrus or flatsedge. Look at the Supplier's list for some suggested sources for pond plants. A good book is *Goldfish Pools, Water Lilies and Tropical Fishes* by Dr. G.L. Thomas Jr., available from Lilly Pons Water Gardens.

Q. We live in a community on a lake that is used for irrigation. When the water level drops, we see ugly pipes and an eroding shoreline. **What can we do to hold the bank and cover the pipes?** Boulders and retainer walls are too expensive.

A. Some attractive native plants are suitable for the edge of the lake or in shallow water. They could help preserve the bank and hide some of the pipes. If a herbicide was used to keep the lake free of aquatic weeds and algae, the herbicide could also kill the plants at the water's edge. I suggest pickerel weed, arrowhead, or spike rush. Spike rush grows densely and can stabilize eroded banks. Aquatic Plant Management in Plantation sells and installs them. Jurassic Wetlands in Okeechobee collects native plants from permitted lands and installs them.

Web sites to visit: The University of Florida: Center for Aquatic and Invasive plants http://aquat1.ifas.ufl.edu

POT AND PATIO PLANTS

Potted plants offer the advantage of portability if they are not too large. Research your plants needs and match them to their proper environment. Anticipate repotting every two years or so with faster growing types. The outdoor location offers a number of advantages including higher humidity, easier pest control, fertilizing and watering, and healthier plants.

Q. **What plants will survive in pots on a sunny, screened patio with minimal care**?
A. I would use tough, sun-tolerant plants that need little water. Purchase big unglazed clay pots with drain holes. The bigger the pot, the longer the plant will not need water or attention. Use a light soil mix to maximize drainage. Good choices include desert rose, dwarf crown-of-thorns, dwarf schefflera, soft-tip yucca, snake plant, jade plant and spider lily. The ti plant, which comes in green, white, red and purple leaf tones, is quite tough and can take some shade and moisture as well as sun and some drought. Ti plants color up better in a sunny location. Fertilize the plant with Peters 20-20-20 according to directions.

Q. I have **an entrance that faces north and receives no sun**. What would look good in that area?
A. Indian hawthorn is a good permanent choice for a large clay pot. It will get 3 feet tall in time and is also salt tolerant. It has small white flowers in the winter and spring.

Q. Why is my *Ficus benjamina* **losing its leaves**? I keep it in a pot on a screened porch overlooking the ocean.
A. I suspect that your ficus could be reacting to the strong winds and minute particles of salt spray coming onto your screened porch. Ficus is not salt tolerant and will defoliate with prolonged heavy wind off the ocean.

Q. My **patio faces north**. What are some suggestions for plantings?
A. A north-facing patio restricts one mainly to foliage plants, although spathyphyllum with white spathes and anthurium with red to pink spathes will provide color most of the year. Impatiens, sultana and torenia are annuals that may work. All of these flowering plants require shelter from cold and wind. Annuals are best between October and April. Summer heat and humidity usually do them in by May. A beautiful elegant patio plant is *Zamia furfuracae*, the cardboard plant. Various ferns should do well with a lot of water. Chinese evergreen, peperomia, pleomele, dracena, dieffenbachia, staghorn fern and many others also will be useful in this location.

Q. What is bothering my **desert rose?**
Your desert rose wants full sun and very little water. It does nicely in a clay pot with good-draining soil such as cactus mix or Pro-mix. It normally loses leaves during the course of the year. Water in the morning only and keep the leaves dry to avoid fungal problems. If flowers do not open properly and the leaves are spotted, use a systemic insecticide such as Orthene. Follow label directions and repeat treatment in ten days. Apply before 10 a.m. Fertilize monthly with Peters 20-20-20.

Q. My patio **faces west and gets full afternoon sun.** What should I plant in the pots against the wall?
A. Try baby sun rose, desert rose or dwarf crown of thorns. These plants propagate easily from cuttings and are used to hot, dry conditions.

Q. What should I do with my **pots of poinsettia?**

A. Poinsettias will do well in the ground in a sunny, fairly dry location in south Florida. Pick a spot where artificial light does not hit the plant (i.e. porch lights, streetlights, etc.) or the blooming cycle will be frustrated. They are short day plants and need the lessening of daylight and cooler temperatures to trigger them into bloom for the holiday season. Fertilize monthly from March to October with a liquid plant food. Water in the morning only to avoid scab, which can severely damage the plants. Keep alert for hornworms, which can strip the foliage during the spring or summer months. Spray with Dipel for control. You may prune the poinsettia for denser growth, but do so no later than mid-June or the blooms will be destroyed.

Q. My **crotons** are in pots on a sunny patio. They are **almost bare and have brown tips on the leaves**. What can I do for better foliage?
A. Crotons experience natural leaf drop, but excessive drop means spider mite activity. Locate the crotons on the patio, out in the open away from overhanging eaves. Natural rainfall usually will wash the mites off. It wouldn't hurt to give them a blast of water from the hose. Insecticidal soap will also work.

Q. My topiary has **sticky leaves** and I don't know what to do.
A. Your topiary is being attacked by a sucking insect. Move it outside to a shady place and treat with Orthene following label directions. Repeat in seven to ten days.

Q. **I would like to grow a coconut on my screened porch**. How do I do this?
A. Coconuts would be unsuitable for a porch because they grow quickly. You cannot collect coconuts and just plant them because they will get lethal yellowing. Instead buy a Malayan dwarf golden coconut grown from certified seed and plant it in the ground. Even the dwarfs can reach 40 feet in height. They like full sun and can spread about 25 feet, so allow plenty of room. Use a smaller palm for your screened porch such as pygmy date palm, which will stay small for many years. The pygmy date prefers a sunny location. If you have a shady porch, try the bamboo palm or lady palm.

Q. The **areca palms** in our pool patio area have turned a rusty brown color. Some are turning yellow while others across the pool remain green. What is happening?

A. Well water can stain arecas a rusty color if sprinklers hit the patio area. Another name for areca palm is yellow butterfly palm. The plants have a yellow-green cast to the foliage in sunny areas. They are greener in the shade. Keep chlorine from the pool away from areca and other plants as it can kill them. You might consider moving them outside. Arecas palms get very large, 25-30 feet tall, and are good for screening out neighbors or bad views. They will get too big for your screened patio. Pygmy date palm, lady palm, and bamboo palm are smaller, slower growers that would do well in a screened area.

Q. We have a new home and would like to add a **low growing plant between stepping-stones**. Will periwinkle, creeping thyme or sedum do well? The location is fairly shady. What will do well in pots on a sunny patio?

A. Some low sedums will do well here but usually need sun. It is too hot for periwinkle and creeping thyme will not last. Mondo grass might be a possibility. Hot patios are perfect for dwarf crown-of-thorns, desert rose and kalanchoes. Use a clay pot for good drainage. All should last a good number of years with little care or watering. Fertilize monthly with Peter's 20-20-20. Be careful with vines, as many grow huge here.

Q. My **topiary plants** came from California and I think they are eugenia. They produced a small cherry-like fruit. What can I do to rescue them as they are going bare?

A. Your plants are *Eugenia myrtifolia* which are popular as topiary plants in California. They make nice small to medium sized trees if allowed to grow out. They are difficult to maintain indefinitely in a topiary form and often go bare on the bottom first. I would use them in the landscape as a tree. They will be almost impossible to restore to the perfect columns they were.

Q. What are these **brown growths** on the back of my **staghorn ferns**? What fertilizer should I use?

A. The brown growths are spore-producing areas and are natural. The staghorn fern can get huge and weigh several hundred pounds. It is best attached to a strong tree like live oak in a shady location.

Banana peels or fruit can be put into the center of the plant to add potassium. If attached to a tree the fern does not need food at all. A half strength application of Peters 20-20-20 applied monthly from March to October can be used if the plant is on a porch or similar location.

ROSES

Roses are challenging in South Florida unless you use the old so-called Florida Cracker roses which are shrubby and have flowers in clusters. Blackspot and powdery mildew are often problems as are spider mites and thrips in the dry season. Roses need full sun and watering every four to five days if there is no rain. Watering should be done in the morning only. If you are in a situation where you cannot control the irrigation, invest in a replacement half or three quarter head to throw water away from your roses. A soaker hose is good as water can slowly ooze out and not get the rose foliage wet. Pick off affected leaves and clean up any foliage on the ground that could harbor fungal spores. These spores can re-infest your plant. Try Polyantha or Floribunda types or the old-fashioned roses like Louis Philippe (red) or Pink Pet (pink) for minimal spraying. Hybrid teas usually require more work. The Cooperative Extension Service has bulletins on rose care.

Q. My **rose bushes** are not doing well. Most have chewed leaves, and one bush is growing under a mango tree. Can I move the bush?
A. Moving old roses is challenging. Be sure to plant roses in a full sun, well-drained, airy location. Dig the new hole first so you can get the rose to the new location quickly to minimize shock. Prune the rose back by at least one-half. Run water on the plant the night before you transplant it so the rootball will stay together. Sandy rootballs often fall apart. Spray with Orthenex to control insects and fungal problems.

Q. My **climbing roses** have lost their lower leaves and have black spots on them. What is wrong?
A. Your roses have blackspot. They need an area that receives at least six hours of sun a day as well as good air circulation and

130

drainage. **Water them with soaker hoses** only in the morning to minimize fungal leaf spot. Spray with Daconil or Funginex for control.

Q. My **wild climbing rose is dropping leaves and has stopped blooming**. What is wrong?
A. Your rose has powdery mildew. For control, spray with copper fungicide, following label directions. Repeat in ten days. Spray only in the morning before 10.

Q.My friend is having **trouble with her rose bushes**. She uses Funginex and Jobs spikes for fertilizer. **Could her rose disease be copper leaf?**
A. Funginex is a good all-purpose fungicide. Water in the morning only and use soaker hoses to reduce fungal problems. Fertilize with a granular rose fertilizer. The spikes concentrate the fertilizer, and you may burn the roots. There is no disease called copper leaf to my knowledge. You may be thinking of rust, which is more common in California and other drier climates.

Q. I have **spider mites and thrips on my roses**. What should I use?
A. Soapy water or Safer's Insecticidal Soap are good controls for these small insects. Systemics like Orthene also give good control. Orthinex combines fungicide and insecticide.

Q. We **want to plant a rose tree** in our community as a tribute to a friend named Rose. I have been to several nurseries and can not find one. Can you help me?
A. The majority of roses require weekly spraying and are too much work for the average residential community on common land. Most maintenance companies come through every two weeks and would not be bothered with rose tree maintenance. Rose trees are grafted on a high-stemmed understock that would also be very prone to blowing over. I would strongly advise against the rose tree concept. Instead, I suggest a shrub type rose that would not require spraying and would be a repeat bloomer. Most of the shrub type roses will get at least 5-6 feet in height over time and would make a nice memorial statement. Some of the better types include 'Carefree Beauty,' 'Carefree Wonder,' 'Louis Philippe,' and 'Old Blush'.

Select a well-drained, open, sunny location. Plant a groundcover like liriope around the rose if it is going to be freestanding in a lawn area. The liriope will keep monofilament trimmers from girdling the rose.

Q. I have a lot of Jackson & Perkins roses that have been **losing leaves**, which I think has been caused by fungus. Our condominium association waters every other day around 3:30 a.m. and has reworked the irrigation system. The sprinklers used to go off at 6:30 a.m. Could this account for the yellowing I am seeing on roses and annuals?
A. Roses want full sun, good air circulation and good drainage. The timing of the sprinklers should not add to the fungal problem. Watering any time between 2 and 10 a.m. is OK. But the water is coming on too often. Once every four days should be fine for established landscapes. The Jackson & Perkins roses are probably grafted to Dr. Huey rootstock, which is susceptible to nematodes. The roses will last about three to four years in the landscape before they die out from nematodes. Fortuniana rootstock is the best for South Florida and can last 30 years or more. Make sure all your roses are grafted on Fortuniana, which resists nematodes. Paying more for these roses is worth it because of longevity.

Q. I would love to plant a **'Blaze' red climbing rose** here. Will the plant do well here? If not what do you suggest?
A. 'Blaze' would have lots of blackspot problems here. Give the rose full sun, good drainage and good air circulation to minimize disease problems. Water in the morning only between 2-10 a.m. I would recommend 'Don Juan' which is a red rose with fragrant larger red flowers and better disease resistance. Make sure it is grafted on Fortuniana rootstock.

Q. Can you recommend **roses for containers**?
A. Old-fashioned roses should do well in large pots and will be much easier than hybrid tea types. Miniature roses are also good.

SALT-TOLERANT PLANTS

Q. **Which** flowers will grow on **an** ocean **high-rise** balcony facing north and northeast?

A. Your choices are very limited. Not many plants will endure the full blast of salt wind with no direct sun. Oceanfront plants like full sun, little water, good drainage and minimal fussing. You might try the following salt-tolerant plants in large pots: sea oxeye daisy, soft-tip yucca, spider lily, dwarf crown of thorns, crinum lily, confederate jasmine vine, railroad vine, Schillings holly, cardboard palm, carissa 'Emerald Blanket', crinum lily, or Indian or Yeddo hawthorn. Flower displays will be modest, but at least these plants have a chance of surviving. The northeast side will receive the worst of the winter winds. Use beach sunflower, gazania or geraniums for window boxes. Keep the soil light and quick draining as most salt-tolerant plants are very subject to root rot.

Q. We live near the ocean and want to put some **large pots** around our pool area. What do you suggest that is **maintenance free**?

A. One attractive combination might be Indian hawthorn in the center of the pot with baby sun rose trailing over the edge. Water large pots about twice a week. Another nice combination could use liriope 'Evergreen Giant' in the center of the pot with 'Aztec Grass' (variegated liriope) around the edge. All are salt tolerant and do not cause maintenance problems.

Q. What shrubs can we **plant along a seawall that gets some salt water?**

A. Scaevola, sea oxeye daisy, beach sunflower and Indian hawthorn are possibilities. These plants like little water once established. I would not plant along a seawall because of the maintenance required. Plant 5-6 feet back from the wall.

Q. My condominium is **on the ocean** and all our plants are brown and look dead. **What can we use**?

A. Ocean front locations are a great challenge because of wind, poor soil, and salt spray. Here are some choices – Palms: Maypan or Malayan dwarf coconuts, hurricane or princess palm,

Washingtonia palm, sabal palm, or thrinax palm. Trees: silver or green buttonwood, noronhia, seagrape (messy), pigeon plum, or live oak. Large shrubs: pittosporum, scaevola, ochrosia, yucca or carissa. Small shrubs: lantana, Shillings holly, or Wheelers pittosporum. Groundcover: lantana, beach sunflower, sea oxeye daisy or beach morninglory.

SHRUBS

Shrubs can offer additional energy savings by shading walls and air conditioners. A shaded air conditioning unit can offer 8% energy savings over one located in the sun. Shrubs serve many important landscape functions including screenings, hedges, accents, foundation plantings, and fragrance and color. Use green plants such as cherry and *Viburnum suspensum* for hedge work. Let flowering plants grow naturally so you can enjoy the blooms, which occur at the branch tips.

Q. Can I save my **crotons from this powdery growth**? I've lost two already.
A. Your crotons have **lichens**, which do not kill the plant. Check the trunk bases for string **trimmer damage**, which can girdle and kill the plants. Crotons can live for many years but have thin bark.

Q. What is causing the leaves of my **pittosporum** to turn a spotted yellow and fade?
A. Pittosporum belongs to a group of plants that prefers drier conditions than they normally receive in the irrigated landscape. Others in this group include citrus, carissa, Texas sage, geranuim, cacti, euphorbia, cassia, queen and areca palms, bird of paradise, royal poinciana, bulnesia, bougainvillea, ligustrum, and most legumes. This is by no means a comprehensive list. Change your watering habits immediately. Pittosporum is subject to root rot. Your leaves have angular leaf spot. Prune out dead branches. Clean up leaves under the plants. Keep mulch away from the base of the plants. Water only in the morning, no more than twice a week. Spray with copper fungicide following label directions and repeat treatment in ten days.

Q. My **juniper has bare spots and looks like it is dried out**. What's wrong?

A. Your variegated juniper has phomopsis; twig blight, which is common on junipers this far south. It occurs most often on plants grown in shady areas or where the shrubs receive a lot of water. Irrigate in the morning only. Keep the plant on the dry side, watering about once every four to five days if there is no rain. Spray twice with copper fungicide at weekly intervals. Juniper needs full sun and good air movement to minimize fungal problems.

SHRUBS - FLOWERING

Q. What are some **good flowering shrubs** to put in my yard?

A. Good flowering shrubs include the large 10'-12' Cape honeysuckle and golden dewdrop. Cape honeysuckle has orange flowers in winter. Golden dewdrop has blue flowers and blooms much of the year. It also gets orange berries that attract birds. Plumbago is a blue flowering smaller shrub to 6'. Hibiscus, 'Nora Grant' ixora, pinwheel jasmine, and thryallis are all good, long-blooming shrubs that you might try for an extended flower display. Stay away from oleander (constant caterpillars) and most ixora (nutritional problems and cold damage) in particular.

Q. What are some suggestions for planting **flowering shrubs on the north side** of our condo?

A. The north side is shady so your plant list is somewhat limited. Most flowering plants need sun to bloom well. If the north side of your condo has no trees in the area you will be able to grow a larger variety of flowering shrubs. Under windows, where you do not want a plant taller than 3 feet or so, I would recommend crossandra, which has orange flowers over the warmer part of the year and grows to about 2 ½ feet tall, or Indian hawthorn which grows to 3 feet, has dark foliage and small white flowers. This is the best low shrub for long term performance. There are pink forms from California that sometimes show up on the market. Brazilian plume flower (*Justicia cornea*) is another short shrub, around 24 inches that blooms well through the summer. All of these plants can be spaced about 18 inches apart. Taller shade lovers include blue sage, which grows 5-6 feet and has pretty blue flowers from December through March. In early April, prune the old flower clusters. Clock bush is a good plant for light shade. It reaches about 7 feet and has beautiful purple trumpet type blooms in spring and winter. Thryallis or shower of gold will bloom in light shade. It has yellow flowers 10 months of the year (rests in January and February) and reaches about 7 feet tall. Crape jasmine has a double and single form available. It is an acid lover, so plant it out from the foundation. The double form is the most available and can reach 8-10 feet in height. It is a faster grower than the single form. Use an azalea/gardenia fertilizer to keep the deep green leaf color. The white flowers occur in spring and summer on the double form. I like the pinwheel jasmine, the single form best. This plant blooms all year and is very slow growing to 6-8 feet. I think it is one of the best plants for sun or shade.

Q. My **pinwheel plants have yellow leaves** and only a few flowers. They have no new growth. Can they be saved?
A. The pinwheel jasmine is a beautiful plant if well grown. Like gardenia, ixora, hibiscus, ligustrum and orange jessamine, it is an acid-loving plant. It should be planted away from concrete side-walks, pool decks and house foundations. It is very subject to chlorosis from high pH. Fertilize with an ixora/gardenia fertilizer. It likes sun to partial shade. Make sure the plant is planted at the same depth it was in the original container. Planting too deep can cause the plant to die back.

Q. I need **a startling, upright, compact plant for a northern corner** of our building that receives only a few hours of sun a day.
A. I would use a colorful foliage plant for a corner location with sparse light. The caricature plant, *Grapophyllum pictum*, comes in a yellow and green leafed form with pretty flowers. The chenille plant, *Acalypa hispida*, has red drooping cattail flowers most of the year and is a conversation piece. The copperleaf, *Acalypha wilkesiana*, has variable-colored leaves, but the red form is the brightest. It sometimes defoliates if the winter is cold for these plants.

Q. **Can I grow azaleas in South Florida?**

A. Azaleas can be grown here with some difficulty. Generally the further north you are in south Florida, the better luck you will have. Azaleas are acid loving plants and south Florida soil is mostly alkaline. Keep them in the shade. If you have live oaks or slash pine on your property, they will grow well under them. Do not plant them near any cement and do not plant too deeply. They have a shallow fibrous root system and dry out quickly, so watch plants for wilting. They benefit from mulching to retain moisture. Use about 50% peat moss well mixed with existing soil when you plant. Fertilize in March, June and October with azalea/gardenia fertilizer. The best varieties for south Florida are: 'Red Wing', a low to medium grower with red flowers; 'Formosa', a tall growing plant with purple flowers; and 'Sweet Surrender', a Formosan type with good alkaline soil tolerance.

Q. I have **azaleas** in all colors and notice the leaves are small. Do they grow tall so that I will have to trim them?

A. Azaleas that get too much sun may have small leaves. Kurume varieties grow about 3 feet tall; Indica types grow 6-8 feet tall. Prune right after flowering for best results

Q. My **gardenia has black stuff on the leaves and is dying**. What is wrong?

A. Sucking insects are attacking your plant. Apply Orthene to the plant according to label directions before 10 a.m. Repeat spray in seven to ten days.

Q. One **part of my gardenia is dying.** Is it trunk die back? I have sprayed with insecticides and use gardenia fertilizer.

A. Your gardenia could have **graft incompatibility**, which would cause a branch to die back. There is no cure.

Q. My **gardenia** has bloomed nicely and now it **is putting out long branches** since repotting. Should I cut these off?

A. Your potted gardenia is probably gardenia 'Radicans', a ground cover also known as the dwarf gardenia. Allow the long branches to develop for more flowers.

Q. I need to find an **early blooming gardenia variety** as I want to enjoy the flowers all year.

A. The small 'veitchii' variety would be a good one to try. It only grows to 4 feet or so and blooms on and off through the year. The flowers are smaller but the fragrance is as good as the big growers. The big variety 'Miami Supreme' will sometimes bloom in the winter as well but will make a bush over 8 feet tall and across. Most nurseries should be able to special order for you. A good gardenia specialty wholesale grower is Carroll's nursery in Clearwater Fl. 1-813-535-5888. Most nurseries order their gardenias for spring sales.

Q. I've seen **hydrangeas** in the supermarkets. Can they be grown near the ocean?

A. Hydrangeas do grow right on the ocean. I have seen them in these locations in Delaware, Cape Cod and Nantucket. The hydrangea will grow in northern Florida, but we do not have enough cold weather for success here. Plants have a northern and southern limit, and hydrangeas range from southern New England to northern Florida in hardiness. You might try Dombeya X 'Seminole' which blooms over the winter and has some resemblance to a hydrangea. Tropical World, a wholesaler in Boynton Beach had them. Have your landscaper or retail nurseryman call about availability for you. My plant blooms from November through April with pinkish-red flower clusters.

Q. I see a lot of **hibiscus** in South Florida. Is it because they are so easy to grow and are problem free?

A. South Floridians love hibiscus because of their beautiful red, yellow, orange, white or pink flowers. But along with the beautiful blooms can come big problems. Gardeners complain of scale, thrips, mealybug, whitefly, nematodes, the loss of leaves, chewed leaves and bud drop. If you, too, are having hibiscus problems, here's some help:

- They need at least six hours of sun to bloom well.
- Fertilize in March, June and October using an acid fertilizer for ixora/gardenia or another product like Lesco 8-10-10 containing manganese and iron. This will encourage growth and bud set.
- Spray only if there is a problem.
- Bud drop can be caused by uneven watering, lack of good sunlight and nutrition or thrips. Thrips are small insects that attack the flower.

- For sucking insects use a systemic like Orthene or Safer's Insecticidal Soap. Never use malathion on hibiscus.
- Spray with a systemic insecticide like Orthene to control thrips, which can prevent proper flower development. Follow label directions and spray before 10 a.m. with a repeat treatment seven to ten days later.
- If leaves are chewed, the culprits could be caterpillars. Apply Sevin or Dipel.
- For scale, use Orthene. You may lose a few leaves, but getting rid of the scale is worth it.
- Select a well-drained location and water no more than twice a week.
- They grow to 8 feet or more, and should not be used where a clipped hedge is required. The flowers bloom at the ends of the branches, and pruning cuts off all the bloom.
- Hibiscus defoliates because of too much water or wind. The root hairs are delicate; if the plant rocks in its pot it may totally defoliate. Winter winds are worst. When the sun gets lower in the sky the plant will not bloom because of lack of light.
- Variegated plants are less vigorous than normal varieties as they do not have as much chlorophyll. This affects plant vigor and can make variegated plants more subject to insect attack.
- To lessen damage from nematodes, look for hibiscus with nematode-resistant rootstock (single red) and use a lot of organic matter in the soil. Organic materials like peat moss repel nematodes.

Q. How do they get all the great **colors of hibiscus**?
A. Most hibiscus are from the Pacific Islands and the Orient. I strongly suspect that the insects that pollinate them in their native lands are not present here. The plant is reproduced here artificially by cuttings and could propagate naturally by layering although this is unlikely because of the upright growth habit. Hibiscus breeders use hand pollination for cross breeding to create the beautiful flowers and colors we see at the hibiscus shows.

Q. I bought a **hybrid hibiscus** at a show and it hasn't bloomed. Why?
A. Your hybrid hibiscus will bloom with time. Show hybrid hibiscus are

often shy bloomers when compared with the old-fashioned single red forms which are in bloom almost daily. The huge flowers on some of the hybrids are up to 7 or 8 inches across and take a lot of energy to produce. Be patient. The blossoms are worth the wait!

Q. When do I transplant **hibiscus**?
A. Hibiscus can be transplanted any time as long as plenty of water is available. Plant them in the ground. Potted plants require a lot more work.

Q. Can I grow **Rose of Sharon as a privacy hedge**?
A. Rose of Sharon is a relative of our hibiscus. I have seen plants here in the ground. They will do reasonably well here although we are somewhat south of their preferred range. Rose of Sharon will tolerate sun to partial shade. It is a large grower to 12 -15 feet tall, so allow plenty of room for its growth. The plant has a growth habit reminiscent of a small tree and tends to be bare at the base, so I wouldn't use it for a privacy hedge.

Q. I want to tell you that the **yesterday-today-and-tomorrow plant** causes shortness of breath, congestion, wheezing and rhinitis. It has a cloying sweet odor that fills the air. You must stay inside or leave the area. Warn your readers.
A. I think yesterday-today-and-tomorrow is getting a bad rap. It is not fragrant; I have a plant in my yard, and I'm allergy-sensitive. I strongly suspect that the **night-blooming jasamine, melaleuca, mango, Brazilian pepper, vitex, angels's trumpet, day jasmine or chalice vine may be in your vicinity. These are the main allergy producers in Florida.**

Q. The maintenance company **hacked back our oleanders** to sticks when they were in full bloom.
A. **I would not prune oleanders** because they are subject to bacterial gall, a fatal disease that is spread from plant to plant by pruning shears. If pruning is done on bacterial gall infested plants, it can be spread to infect other oleanders on the property. Bacterial gall shows up as swellings on the stems and dead shoots above. You must dip pruning tools in alcohol between each cut. The oleander is woody in nature and does not regenerate well from

repeated cuttings. It naturally is bare of foliage at the base so it is best to let it grow naturally as a background shrub and plant something low in front. Oleanders attract caterpillars, scale and gall. They should be used far away from buildings so the flowers can be observed at a distance and their faults will not be so obvious.

Q. **How do I root a plant** like oleander?
A. Oleanders can be rooted from cuttings cut at a diagonal across the stem. The cuttings are branch tips about 4-6 inches long. Strip the bottom leaves off the cuttings and dip the ends of the cuttings into a rooting hormone like Rootone. Put the cutting in a light potting soil mix or half sand and half peat moss mix. Put the plants on the north side of the house or under a tree where the direct sun does not hit them. Keep cuttings moist but not soggy. They should root as new plants within two to three months. Then gradually move them into more sun. Eventually you can plant them into the ground after five or six months when they are well rooted.

Q. I am looking for **something with blue blossoms and easy care** to plant in my yard.
A. **Plumbago** is one of the subtopic's few blues. It requires little care. It likes sun to filtered shade. Water established plants one to twotimes a week if there is no rain. Plumbago can spread about 5-6 feet over time. New leggy shoots lean over, branch and flower, so do not cut them off and it will spread .
Q. I have a large stand of **plumbago** about 20 years old. They give off fewer and fewer flowers. What fertilizer and water do they need? Can I cut them back drastically?
A. Plumbago does well with an ixora/gardenia fertilizer applied in March, June, and October. Do not cut them back drastically unless it is absolutely necessary. When I had my house painted, I cut my plumbago to the ground to provide access for the painter. The plumbago is now 6 feet tall and looks fine. However, this radical pruning would not normally be recommended on most plants. Plumbago has the ability to come back from the roots with few problems, so it worked in my case. In most instances, I would only remove a third of the total growth. Remove dead or old wood to let new growth renew the plant. June or July is the best time for heavy pruning as the plant has cloud cover to protect it from sunscald and

it will recover quicker in the summer months.

Q. Will **butterfly bush and lemon grass** grow in Palm Beach County?
A. Butterfly bush and lemon grass do grow there.

Q. I planted some **dwarf ixora**s in front of my house and they died in two months. I would like another suggestion on what to use. I thought **arborvitae** or the **yews** from the north as possible replacements. Can yews grow here?
A. Stay away from arborvitae as they age poorly here and can get to be 25 feet tall and as wide. Yews will not grow here as we are too far south. The big pink 'Nora Grant,' 'Super King' and *Ixora coccinea* varieties normally do not have flowering problems if they receive at least 4-5 hours of direct sun. I find the dwarf ixora troublesome as they are subject to nematodes and get chlorotic. Plant any new plantings out beyond the drip line of the roof. Space big ixoras 2 to 2 ½ feet apart and smaller plants 1 ½ feet apart. Remember that flowering plants bloom at the ends of the branches so cut only off extra tall shoots so you do not ruin your flower display. Keep the acid-loving ixoras away from alkaline concrete sidewalks and buildings because this causes a great deal of stress on the plants. The concrete's alkalinity leaches into the nearby soil as the building or walkway weathers. Our soils are generally alkaline to begin with so the concrete intensifies the problem. They will need an acid fertilizer in March, June and October.

Q. I have **brown leaves on my 'Maui' ixora. Is that leaf spot?**
A. Fungal leaf spot indicates your plant received too much water or that water was applied at the wrong time. Water only between 2 and 10 a.m. to minimize fungal problems. Copper fungicide is used to control leafspot. 'Maui' ixora can be attacked by microscopic worms called nematodes, which can cause leaves to brown off and look bad. 'Maui' only last three to four years because the nematodes kill them. Do not replace them with other 'Maui' ixora.

Q. The **leaves on my ixora are covered with a black mold**. What do I do to clean them?
A. Your ixora has sooty mold, a fungal by-product growing on the

honeydew created by sucking insects. The sucking insects are most likely scale or mealybug. Try soapy water – two teaspoons of liquid dishwashing soap to a gallon of water. Spray the mixture on the affected area, particularly along the stems and on the undersides of leaves. Repeat weekly for two additional applications. You can also use a systemic insecticide like Orthene for control.

Q. How do you **propagate crown-of-thorns**? How big do they grow and do they have bad roots?
A. Propagate crown-of-thorns from branches 6 inches long. Let the branches dry for a day before sticking them in an unglazed pot with cactus soil mix. They propagate best between March and July. The big varieties grow to 4-5 feet in height. The dwarfs grow to 3 feet tall. Neither has invasive roots.

Q. Can you tell me where to obtain **the big crown-of-thorns**? All the nurseries only seem to sell the mini types.
A. Big varieties of crown-of-thorns have bigger leaves and can grow to at least 4-5 feet tall. 'American Beauty' is one of the big varieties. My objection to these plants is that they have a tuft of leaves and flowers on top and lots of exposed thorny stems which does not exactly make them attractive. The dwarfs stay much tighter in growth without all the ugly exposed stems. I have seen the big variety at several nurseries; ask your local nursery to get them for you. As the plants grow they will eventually reach the 5-foot height range. They need full sun and minimal water.

Q. Our **crown-of-thorns** has gotten leggy and seems to have lost its color. Why?
A. Yours may be either planted too deep or be in a low spot in the bed where the water doesn't drain off quickly. **Keep crown-of-thorns very dry.** They can get root rot and fungal problems from too much water. Crown-of-thorns loves sun and if your plants are at the shady end of the bed that can also cause them to be off color and more leggy

Q. I have tried **rooting hibiscus** and have not been successful. How can I make it root?
A. You probably attempted rooting at the wrong time of the year.

Cuttings can be rooted from June through August with good success.

Q. Can you tell me about **wild coffee** and where I can get this plant?

A. Wild coffee is an understory plant that grows in the hammock areas of south Florida. Its red berries are attractive and resemble the common coffee fruit. Wild coffee normally grows to 5 feet in height. Sources include Native plant nurseries and Native Plant Society sales.

Q. I miss my lilacs. Can I grow **lilac bushes in south Florida**?

A. Lilacs are not suited to south Florida. They cannot tolerate the prolonged heat and humidity of the summer. Lilacs also must have an extended cold season to thrive. They grow as far south as the mountains of South Carolina and Georgia. They are very cold tolerant and are hardy quite far north to Canada. Use great caution in ordering from mail order sources. We are located in Zone 10 and 11 on most hardiness maps. Most mail order nurseries serve wide areas of the country and have few things geared for this area. However, one reader said she had a lilac bush. She picked the leaves off the plant in early November to simulate winter and watered with ice water over the winter months. She let the plant leaf out again in March. I think her plant will eventually die. It seems like plant abuse to me. I would suggest visiting local botanical gardens to become familiar with the beautiful plants that you can grow down here. You can also invest in plant books at local nurseries or in the gift shops at these gardens to help you in selecting plants for the area. It is exciting when you think that the lilac blooms maybe two weeks up north whereas here you can have plants in bloom year round. Crape myrtle might be a good substitute for a lilac as the flowers are very similar, but not fragrant. They bloom from June to October and come in shades of white, pink, red, fuschia and purple.

Q. I saw a beautiful plant called **mussaenda**. Can you tell me where is the best place to plant it?

A. Mussaenda is spectacular in the warm months with colorful bracts of pink or white. This large shrub goes bare over the winter and is very tropical so it should be placed where it has protection from winter winds. It takes sun to partial shade.

Q. You mentioned some time ago that **tibouchina** was a difficult plant for south Florida. Ours is doing well. We give it lots of water

A. Congratulations on growing a difficult plant successfully. My viewpoint is based on lots of observations over the years. These Brazilian plants like acid soil to do well. Most of our soil is alkaline so they are challenging at best. Fertilize with an acid fertilizer for ixoras and gardenias in March, June and October. Your tibouchina has large purple flowers and fuzzy leaves and is *Tibouchina semidecandra* or glory bush. The small tree form does better here and is called the purple glory tree, *Tibouchina granulosa*. Both types do better in interior areas of the counties with the heavier muck type soil.

Some web sites to visit:
The American Hibiscus Society at http://www.trop-hibiscus.com
Florida Plants Online at http://www.floridaplants.com

SUCCULENTS

Succulents can be potted or grow in the ground. Most require a lot of sun and excellent drainage. In -ground plants do fine without extra water. They often do best if planted on a sandy mound. Potted plants should be grown in a cactus soil mix for good drainage. Unglazed clay pots offer an extra measure of insurance against over-watering. Water only in the morning if it is required. Succulents are very prone to fungal problems and **excess watering can easily kill them**.

Q. I have a **cactus** that is growing wild in my small condo garden. Can it be replanted?
A. The cactus can be replanted and probably is not suitable for a small condo yard. See if the grounds committee will OK transplant-

ing it to a large landscape. It needs to be out in an open, sunny dry area away from people.

Q. I need to **repot my cactus**. What is the best way?
A. I would wear good thick gloves when working with cacti. They require a sandy, sharp draining soil, full to part sun, and very little water. A clay pot or dish would be best. Make sure it is unglazed for good air circulation and drainage. Put a layer of stone in the bottom to insure good drainage but do not block the drain hole. A layer of sphagnum moss over the stones separates the soil from the stones to prevent the soil from washing down the hole. Use a very light soil mix or mix the potting soil with 50% builders sand to insure good aeration. Most regular potting soils are too heavy for cactus growth. Fertilize every two months between March and October with a liquid houseplant fertilizer

Q. My **catcus has scale**. What should I use to get rid of it?
A. Use Orthene and repeat the treatment in seven to ten days. You can take a hose and blast the cactus stems and wash off the dead scale. Living scale do not come off easily and you can see fresh feeding damage if you flick them off.

Q. My **aloe has turned a reddish brown**. Is it dying?
A. When aloe foliage turns a reddish brown it is usually the oldest lower leaves and they are preparing to dry up and die. This is a natural condition and I would remove the oldest leaves that are affected.

Q. I planted buds from a **burro's tail** but they don't seem to be growing. What is the problem?
A. The burro's tail or donkey's tail is a type of sedum that likes bright conditions and little water. It is extremely brittle. The trailing branches can be broken off and rooted fairly easily. Remove the bottom leaves from a 2-inch shoot and insert it into a light potting soil mix. Use Peters 20-20-20 or other liquid fertilizer at half strength to assist the rooting process. The best time to get new shoots is in April or May. Keep the soil fairly moist during the first five to six weeks to promote rooting. After that ease off on watering. Burro's tail has small delicate roots that

are prone to root rot. . Putting the plant into brighter light conditions should improve its color, too.

Q. We would like to plant a **night-blooming cactus**. Do you have any suggestions?
A. Cereus like an open, dry spot. Some of the Peruvian types can reach 20 feet tall, so don't plant it under wires. Cereus usually have spectacular 8-inch white flowers that open at night and are very fragrant.

Q. What is causing holes in my **yucca**?
A. It may have a yucca stem borer which can tunnel through the stem and destroy the plant. Probe in the holes with a wire to impale the borer if possible. Dursban may be of some help if sprayed on the stems and around the holes. Yuccas like the same conditions as crown of thorns…full sunlight and dry. Water in the morning only.

 **Christmas Cactus**

Q. I have a **holiday cactus**. I don't know how to tell which one it is or how to care for it.
A. There are three Schumbergera cultivars commonly seen in cultivation. They normally bloom at either **Thanksgiving, Christmas or Easter,** depending on the species. The Christmas cactus has scalloped margins on the segments and blooms at the tip only. The Easter cactus blooms at the stem tips and between the stem segments. The Thanksgiving or crab cactus blooms at the stem tips and has two to four pointy teeth along the margins of the stem segments. Keep your cactus in a bright light on a porch or patio area or under a tree. Direct sun could scorch the plant. Fertilize with a good liquid soluble fertilizer monthly from March to October. Do not fertilize over the winter months. These cacti are all short day plants. They need cool temperatures (in the 50's) and shorter day length to set buds and trigger bloom. Keep your plant away from artificial light for about six weeks in October and November to initiate bloom. Artificial light includes interior lighting, streetlights, etc. that could interrupt the day length sequence. After bud set do not move the plants as the buds can easily drop off if disturbed. They do not need repotting too often as they

147

have a small root system. Use a clay pot and a sharp draining potting soil that does not have too much peat moss to avoid root rot. Water when the top half of the soil is dry in the pot. Drain off excess water at the bottom of the plant. These cacti grow on trees in Brazil.

Q. My **Christmas cactus has brown growths on the stems and** it is falling apart. What is wrong?
A. It looks like the cactus has odema which causes swelling growth and weak stems. I would restart the plant from healthy shoots and cut back on watering. Do not water until the soil feels totally dry.

Q. I want to buy a **pencil cactus**. Can you help me locate one?
A. Pencil cactus does well outdoors. Be careful of the milky poisonous sap. Many nurseries do not carry the plant any more because of this. However, some might special order it for you.

Q. Our condominium board planted **cactus plants along the walkway** to the parking area a few years ago. They have grown very big and stick out into the walkway. One at the end has sharp points on the ends and I'm afraid someone is going to get hurt. Do you think we should move them?
A. Your cactus sounds like an agave or century plant. Most yuccas also have dangerous points at the ends of the leaves. They are hard to transplant, as the root systems are quite deep. Some agaves spread by a suckering root system. Most put up a huge flower spike in 10 to 15 years and then die. New suckers or offsets continue the plants after the mother plant dies. These plants are not appropriate along walkways. A potential lawsuit is a real possibility for the condominium if an injury occurs. At a minimum, all points should be removed from the plants near walkways. Transplanting to an open area would be the best solution. The plants are not poisonous, but the spines can cause a festering puncture wound.

TREES - ARBORISTS

You can easily spend hundreds or thousands of dollars on tree care and want to make sure the job is done right. Be wary of weekend pruning jobs by unlicensed hackers in an unmarked pickup truck Arborists should be licensed and insured with the state and be certified arborists. The certification means they have received training in correct pruning practices and should be able to do a decent pruning job on your trees. Certification is done annually and classes are held to update arborists in new techniques or changes that have taken place in the past year. Membership in arborists associations indicates a commitment by the company to maintain high standards in the industry. The International Society of Arboriculture is one such group that maintains a list of certified arborists. This business is very changeable with companies going in and out of business rapidly. Shop carefully before you choose a company. Beware of ads advertising topping or other hat rack pruning techniques. Your city or county landscape inspectors may have brochures available on correct pruning techniques. The Cooperative Extension Service in each county will also have good brochures on pruning. Educate yourself before spending a lot of money.

TREES – CITRUS

In Florida almost everyone wants a citrus tree in the yard. They are wonderful to look at and delicious to devour. Most require very little care. Most of the problems that might occur, branch dieback, fruit split, peeling bark, borer attack, root rot and eventual death are all the result of excess watering. Citrus can be watered once every two and a half to three weeks if there is no rain. I would put half-heads on the sprinklers system to throw the water away from the trees. Fertilize in March, June and October with a good citrus fertilizer and enjoy your bounty!

Q. My **pink grapefruit** has a **bitter taste** and is 11 years old. What is wrong?

A. Excess watering definitely affects the taste of the fruit. Stop all irrigation permanently within the tree's root zone. Cut out any dead wood. The tree could be grafted to sour orange rootstock. If the fruit does not improve in taste with elimination of the water, the sour orange rootstock has overtaken the tree and crowded out the pink grapefruit.

Q. My **navel orange has dry fruit with a thick skin**. What is wrong?

A. The navel tree with dry, thick-skinned fruit has been watered too much. It is best to cap sprinkler heads permanently near the citrus root system because they can get fatal root rot if irrigated along with the lawn. Use half heads to throw water away from the trees if the heads are to the edge of the tree canopy. Citrus need water only if there has not been rain for about three weeks. Then you can use a hose for watering. Most years the trees do fine on the rainfall that nature provides. This is true for established trees in the ground two years or more

Q. My nine-year-old **tangelo** had many flowers and just a **few fruit**. Do you have any idea why this is?

A. Tangelos may produce heavily one year and take a break the following year. This is known as alternate bearing and is common on some apple trees as well.

Q. My **grapefruit** tastes fine but has an **ugly spotted skin**. What can be done for this condition?

A. The skin has melanose, a fungal condition. It is unattractive, but does not affect the fruit's taste. Cut off any dead wood. Permanently cap sprinklers under the tree's root zone to reduce the melanose condition and avoid root rot.

Q. My 20-year-old **grapefruit's leaves are curled up and have black dots underneath**. We can't control the sprinklers. It is blooming now and has good fruit. Can we save it?

A. Your grapefruit appears to be suffering from leaf miners and some scale. Do not spray when the tree is in bloom. Spray with Safer's Insecticidal Soap on the undersides of the leaves.

Q. My **grapefruit has holes in it about 1 inch deep**. What causes this problem?

A. Grapefruit holes are caused by shield-shaped insects called stinkbugs. Harvest fruit early to avoid this pest. Stinkbugs are very mobile, so spraying is pretty useless. Normally they damage only a few fruits and there are plenty left over for the family and friends. The small bugs in the fruit are scavengers and help to dispose of it. They are nature's garbagemen.

Q. **What is eating my young two-year-old citrus leaves**? I tried soap spray to no avail.

A. Sevin is about the only spray safe for insects chewing on citrus leaves. Chances are it is nocturnal caterpillars, leaf cutter bees or beetles chewing on the foliage. Damage is very minor from chewing insects, so I am not inclined to worry excessively about them. I personally would not spray. If you do spray, follow label directions exactly. **Do Not Spray if the plants are blooming**. Sevin is lethal to bees. If the bees are killed - no pollination - no fruit. Use Thuricide for caterpillars.

Q. My grapefruit tree has **exposed roots**. Should they be covered?

A. You can cover the roots of the tree with extra soil from around the yard as long as you do not add too much. More than an inch or so can cause plants to decline as oxygen is cut off from the roots.

Q. We did not have a big crop from our grapefruit tree last year. Neighborhood **children climb the tree and swing from the branches. Will this affect the tree?**

A. Children swinging and climbing in the tree can certainly affect the crop. The shaking of the branches will affect pollination and will cause fruit to fall prematurely.

Q. **We have a 12-foot thorny citrus** that finally produced this bumpy fruit with little juice. **What is it?**

A. Your fruit is rough lemon, which is used as an understock for the fancy citrus top. The understock can sucker around ground level, outgrow the fancy top and shade it out. I think this is what happened to your tree. You can remove it or prune it into a small flowering tree where the sharp thorns will not hurt anyone.

Q. We have a **Valencia orange tree** in our yard that has produced a **seedling**. If I plant it in another part of the yard will I get more of the same wonderful tasting fruit?

A. Your young orange seedling was cross-pollinated with another citrus tree to produce your seedling. After six or seven years you should have a tree old enough to bear oranges. Because we do not know what the other parent is, we cannot predict what the fruit will taste like. Chances are it will be okay. Grafting a Valencia shoot to the seedling is the only sure way of reproducing the Valencia qualities you desire. Grafting is usually done in April or May.

Q. We just moved to Florida and are anxious to plant some fruit trees in our yard. **My husband says we should plant fruit trees at least 5 feet apart. What do you say?**

A. Five-foot spacing between trees is way too close for any fruit tree to develop properly. The fastest, biggest tree will reach for the light and shade and kill out the other trees through competition. Fruit trees need sun to produce a good crop. Before the other trees ultimately die out; they will be too shaded to set fruit. The remaining tree will be tall and leggy and you will need a tall ladder to get the fruit. **Minimum spacing on citrus is** 15 feet apart on Meyer lemon, kumquat, and Key lime; 20 feet apart on oranges, tangelos and tangerines; 25 feet apart on grapefruit, and 30 feet or more on avocados and mangos.

Q. I have **an orange tree that is producing fruit and flowers at the same time**. Is this unusual?

A. Young citrus trees often flower and fruit when they are in a stress condition, such as in a container with crowded roots. They may also bloom and fruit initially after planting out in the yard. The young trees often need a few years to establish good root systems and make enough top growth to support a good crop.

Q. **Why didn't my citrus tree produce fruit that was as tasty as the fruit I had last year ?**

A. Citrus produce varying crops each year depending on weather, rainfall, pollination, etc. It is like farming and each year is different.

Q. I have **a citrus bush with fruit between an orange and lemon**.

The fruit is more yellow and the bush is thorny. What is it?
A. The half lemon/orange is probably sour orange, which is good for marmalade and as a meat sauce for barbecue.

Q. Can you recommend **a good variety of tangerine**?
A. Good tangerine varieties include 'Dancy' and 'Mineola'.

Q. My Key lime **fruit drops off when it is the size of a pea**. What is happening?
A. Key lime and other fruit trees will abort fruit that cannot carry to term. Young trees and underfertilized trees are most likely to abort fruit.

Q. My ten-year old lemon tree is suffering **from loss of foliage, particularly on one side**. I fertilize and sprayed with malathion when I noticed the leaves getting sparse. It receives some water from the sprinkler system but not a lot. What else could be the problem?
A. You didn't mention insects, so it may be one or a combination of reasons that caused your tree to decline. Your tree **could have been girdled with a weed trimmer**, which will kill the tree slowly over time. Plant a ground cover such as liriope around the tree trunk to act as a buffer between the weed trimmer and the trunk. The tree **may be planted too deep**. Tree trunks should show a widened flare where they enter the ground if they are planted at the right depth. Trees planted too deep will have trunks that enter the ground vertically like a telephone pole. Dig carefully with a trowel to the flare on the trunk. Remove excess soil from over the root system to about 3 feet from the trunk until it looks like a dished plate with the tree in the center. This will allow roots to breathe and the tree to recover if it is not too far gone. Because one side of the tree had sparse foliage **it could indicate girdling roots.** If the roots were potbound when purchased, they will wrap in a spiral around the original root ball. As the trunk expands, it contacts the spiraling roots and cannot grow more. This can stress one side of the tree and cause leaf and fruit drop. The girdling root has to be carefully dug out and cut off. **Citrus also suffer from root rot in a lawn setting with regular irrigation**. Trees with root rot have splitting, poor tasting fruit; poor foliage, branch dieback and splitting bark

borers. They eventually die.

Q. My grapefruit is **dropping a lot of leaves** now (March). Is this normal for this time of year?
A. Yes, leaf drop is normal for March. Vigorous new growth and flowers also should be appearing now. If the tree has lost more than three quarters of its leaves at one time, I would suspect root rot and excess water.

Q. We live on a canal that has a seawall in the backyard. **How close to the seawall can I plant a t**ree?
A. Keep your trees away from the seawall. These tend to lose soil behind them and need constant repair work. Set the trees at least 6 to 8 feet from the wall.

TREES - OTHER FRUIT

Q. We have a grafted **avocado** planted in 1988. It **sets small fruit that all drop off**. We water and feed regularly, apply dormant oil spray and insecticide before blooming. How can we get fruit to set?
A. Stop using the dormant oil and insecticidal sprays unless there is a specific pest problem. Never spray anything when the plant is in flower. Water the tree no more than twice a week or the fertilizer will be leached through the soil before the tree can use it. Some fruit drop is normal. Increase the fertilizer so the tree has the energy to carry the fruit to maturity.

Q. My **avocado has brown leaves that drop off**. I have sprayed with all kinds of combinations of Sevin and malathion. What can I do?
A. Sevin and malathion are deadly to bees, which are the pollinating insects. No bees mean no fruit. Thrips and spider mites have attacked your avocado. These sucking insects can cause leaf drop but usually do not affect the crop. Mites attack during hot dry weather. They can cause leaf drop and a rusty appearance to the avocado fruit. The fruit is still good. Try Safer's Insecticidal Soap

spray for control. Use only organic products on edibles. Systemic insecticides poison the entire plant including the fruit. Safer Inc. offers a brochure that opens into a handy chart suitable for hanging. It covers many organic controls for weeds and insects that are safe and non-toxic. This should be very valuable for all gardeners concerned with the environment. It is available free; send a SASE to Safer Gardens. (See supplier's list for address)

Q. My **avocado** was planted from seed in 1994 and it blossomed this year. It didn't set any fruit. **Does it need another tree for pollination,** or is it too young?

A. Avocados take eight to ten years before they bear fruit, and fruit from seed-grown trees may not taste exactly like the parent plant because of cross-pollination. Avocados can be morning or after-noon bloomers, and usually need another avocado nearby for cross-pollination in order to set reliable fruit. Other factors like weather can affect fruit production. Bees do not pollinate in windy or rainy weather, so crops are highly variable from year to year. They are somewhat brittle trees, so it is best to grow them well away from the house.

Q. My **avocado tree has developed some strange looking flat-tened stems**. I am concerned about the tree and want to know what I should do about it.

A. Your avocado has developed fasciation, which is an abnormal proliferation of cells causing the stems to become flattened. I have a cassia tree in my yard that does the same thing. Faciated branches will often flower and fruit more, so they should be left on the tree. They may look strange, but the tree is not damaged by the unusual growth pattern. Celosia and a willow known as the fantail willow develop a similar condition. The fantail willow's flattened branches are in great demand by flower arrangers.

Q. My 25- year old '**Coquette' avocado** has loads of fruit but they are small and hard as a rock and have not ripened. What do you advise?

A. I would advise thinning out the crop which will be less of a strain on the tree and should result in larger fruit. Trees that overbear are weakened and need extra fertilizer to recover. The energy of the tree has been sapped producing so many small fruit. Cooler weather may help with the ripening.

Q. Is the **sapodilla** a hearty tree?
A. The sapodilla is a good tropical fruit tree that holds up against strong wind. The fruit was used for chicle in chewing gum and can be eaten fresh. It is brown and soft when ripe.

Q. Our **mango** has delicious fruit. Should we harvest it while it is green or wait until it ripens on the tree?
A. Allow some fruit to ripen on the tree and pick some while green. Extension Service offices have recipes for both green and ripe mangoes. You can ripen the green fruit in a paper bag with an apple in it. The apple gives off ethylene gas, which will help to ripen the fruit.

Q. My young **mango** dropped all its fruit when it was half grown. What can I do to prevent this?
A. Grafted mangos need to be four to five years old before they set fruit. Seedling trees may take eight to ten years. The trees may not have been old enough or had enough nutrition to carry the fruit to term. The older the tree, normally the better the crop. Use citrus/avocado fertilizer in March, June and October to encourage fruit yields.

Q. Our 46-year-old Hayden **mango** has been diagnosed with **anthracnose**. It needs to be sprayed with copper fungicide. When should it be sprayed? Who should I get to spray, and how much will it cost?
A. Anthracnose is a fungus that causes twig cankering and dieback, spotted dropping leaves and spotted fruit with bad areas. Anthracnose is difficult to completely control. Many people simply live with it, but it does affect fruit quality and the mango foliage always has brown edges. Certain mangos are quite resistant; the Philippine types such as Saigon, Cecil, and Cambodia are not very susceptible to anthracnose and produce good quality fruit. To control anthracnose use copper fungicide, Zineb or Maneb, weekly from just before the flowers open to fruit set. Afterward spray monthly till mid-May for early varieties and mid-June for late varieties. The

copper can stain objects blue, so caution should be used when applying. The larger the tree, the higher the cost. Call at least three pest-control companies for estimates. They may have to see your job before giving you a price. Most mangos grow 50 to 60 feet, and most hose sprayers will reach only to about 20 feet. If you want a dwarf variety that grows to only 20 feet, try 'Julie'.

Q. I had an **edible fig tree** in Long Island that grew well and produced fruit. We have some potted small trees and I would like to try one here. Will the fig grow here, and what care does it need?
A. Edible figs are a bit south of their best growing conditions in South Florida. 'Brown Turkey' is one of the best varieties for this climate and grows to about 15 feet. Plant in an open location in full sun with good air movement and drainage. To minimize nematode damage keep the tree permanently mulched to a depth of at least 2 inches. Keep the mulch at least 1 inch away from the stems. Water in the morning only between 2 and 10 a.m. Keep water off the leaves if possible. Figs like good air movement to minimize the rust disease, which causes the leaves to fall off. When you see reddish spots on the leaves, spray with copper fungicide, following label directions. Repeat treatment in 10 days. Fertilize with citrus fertilizer in March, June and October.

Q. How can I get my **figs to ripen** once they are off the tree?
A. Put the figs in a bag with an apple after you pick them from the tree. This should ripen them up in a few days time as the ethylene gas from the apple stimulates ripening.

Q. I planted a **carambola** seed that I got at Mounts Botanical Garden. I put it near the house. It has grown to 7 feet tall. How should I care for it?
A. I certainly would move it out from the house wall into an open area where it will have room to develop properly. Most tropical fruit trees will grow to 30 feet tall and need lots of space and light. Look for fruit after about eight years. Feed with citrus fertilizer in March, June and October.

Q. My **papaya** has bugs in it. What can I do to stop them from getting into the fruit?

A. Papaya fruit fly is a major pest in this area. Spraying is not effective. Some success has been reported bagging the fruit with heavy brown bags. The small fruit fly cannot penetrate the bag and fruit to lay its eggs, which hatch out into worms. Do not use plastic bags. The fruit will rot and turn to mush under a plastic bag. You have to love papaya to go to all that trouble. Research is trying to develop a thick-skinned papaya that the fruit fly cannot penetrate, so there may be hope in the future.

Q I have a mastwood tree. I don't know much about the tree or it's fruit. **If squirrels eat the fruit it does that mean I can eat it too?** A. Your trees are **calophyllum, commonly called beautyleaf or mastwood**. Calophyllum is strong wooded and fairly salt tolerant. The fruit shouldn't harm the squirrels, but should **not** be eaten by humans. Calophyllum is very sensitive to cold, so it may suffer some dieback in cold winters.

Q. My young 'Mauritius' **lychee** tree is 12 feet tall and has brown-tipped leaves. I feed it 6-6-6, Epsom salts and Milorganite in March, June and October. I am not sure how much to use. What causes the brown tips and is my fertilizer mix OK?
A. It would be better to use a regular citrus fertilizer, which would be higher in minor elements and more appropriate for the tree. Follow label directions on the fertilizer bag for application rates. I usually sprinkle the fertilizer lightly and evenly like salt on a hamburger, starting 1 foot from the trunk and fertilizing out to about 2 feet beyond the outermost branch spread. You can then water the fertilizer into the soil for 10 minutes or apply before a rainstorm. The Milorganite is mostly nitrogen and the Epsom salts is magnesium, which is one of the minor elements. The times you fertilize are fine. The 'Mauritius' variety fruits on a more regular basis than the 'Brewster' variety, which often fruits only every three or four years. The lychee leafs out early in the year and foliage is subject to windburn or cold damage as it emerges. The tree gets hardier as it grows older, but needs protection from the wind. The brown tips seem like standard equipment but the more balanced citrus fertilizer should help. Lychee seems to like damp conditions with an even supply of water through the year. Mulch the tree to help water retention, but keep mulch 1-2 inches away from the

trunk. Water the tree about twice a week if there is no rain. Lychees seem to like the inland muck soils better than the sandy soils along the coast.

Q. You mentioned **a chutney tree** on your radio show and I want to get one but I don't know what to ask for?

A. You are looking for the **Indian tamarind**, which lasts in strong hurricane winds. It produces edible pods used in chutney and is a good, long-loved shade tree.

Q. Are **bananas** easy to grow in South Florida?

A. Yes. They like full sun, a somewhat moist location, and abundant fertilizer. Bananas also like a good permanent mulch around the base of the clump. Recycling old banana leaves and using them for the mulch is a good idea as the leaves are high in phosphorous. Use a citrus fertilizer on bananas in March, June, and October. Water plants when it is dry. Bananas can form within 20-24 months after emergence of shoots from the ground. This happens only if they are well fed. Cut the old stems down after fruiting. New shoots continue the production cycle.

Q. Something is eating my **bananas**. They have holes in them. What should I do?

A. Bananas are not normally troubled by many insects. If fruit is left on the tree too long, various scavenger beetles will feed on it. These are normally considered good guys, like nature's garbage men. Try to pick your fruit as soon as it becomes ripe.

Q. Can I grow **a cherry tree** in South Florida?

A. Cherry trees do not grow this far south. North Georgia is about as far south as they go. You might try **Barbados cherry**, which has a cherry-like appearance and a nice tart flavor

Q. I have a **jaboticaba** that is going on six years old. I've not gotten any fruit. What should I do?

A. Jaboticabas are very slow growing and also slow to fruit. I've seen plants in containers fruiting at 6 feet. When they finally get started, they can fruit four or five times a year. Keep the tree mulched. It bears well in sun to partial shade. I normally recommend a citrus/acid type fertilizer like a 4-6-8 to encourage fruiting in March, June and October. You might supplement this with a half strength liquid application of a bloom special to try initiating flowers and fruit. Jaboticaba probably belongs in a class in with some other ornery blooming plants. Wisteria vines in the north are famous for being erratic bloomers. My *Tabebuia avellande* is in the same class at the moment. It is growing madly, but puts out only a few blossoms. In Europe fruit growers sometimes partially girdle branches to stimulate fruiting, but I think this is a bit radical.

Q. Can you eat the fruit from a **loquat tree**?
A. Loquats are edible and considered quite good. The Cooperative Extension Office should have a loquat brochure available. Loquats get fireblight once in a while. The branch tips will die back. The best thing to do is prune out the dead wood. Loquat is otherwise pretty pest free.

Q. I purchased a **breadfruit tree** in the Keys. How do I care for it in (Palm Beach)?
A. Breadfruit is a very tender tropical tree that can be grown in Key West and the Lower Keys. It cannot endure any freezing temperatures, so will not survive on the Florida mainland.

Q. What can you tell me about **Jambolayan plum**?
A. Jambolayan plum is a large growing tree with very strong wood. It produces fruit heavily, probably more than the average home-owner can use. The Cooperative Extension Office has brochures on fruit tree care and recipes for exotic fruits. The Rare Fruit and Vegetable Council is a good organization that provides interesting lectures on tropical fruits and features taste tables where you can experience some fine tropical delicacies.

Q. How do you handle a **macadamia tree**?
A. Macadamia trees can be handled like citrus. They are more tolerant of water than citrus so are not subject to root rot. Fertilize in March, June and October with a citrus/avocado fertilizer. Spread the fertilizer evenly over the ground from about 1-foot from the base of the tree to the outermost branch spread known as the drip line. Macadamia trees set a good crop if there is another macadamia nearby for cross-pollination. The trees often set more fruit than

they can bring to term, so many are dropped early. This is true of citrus, peaches, apples and other fruit and nut trees.

Q. I would like to purchase **a kumquat tree**. How should I care for it?
A. Kumquat is handled the same way as other citrus.

TREES – FLOWERING

The flowering trees that bloom in summer are some of our most brilliant and beautiful. Skeptical? Just take a look at **the royal poinciana**, a large tree with showy clusters of flowers ranging in color from bright orange to red. Known as the 'Flamboyant' in most tropical countries, it typically blooms in South Florida in June and July, but some years by the middle of May. Tthe royal poinciana's flowers appear on bare branches after a two-to-three-month resting stage that is caused by the dry season. Individual flowers can be 4 to 5 inches across and are produced in large clusters that smother the crown of the tree. The big, umbrella-shaped crown is beautiful if adequate space is available to accommodate it. This is a tree for big lots, parks and boulevards. In confined situations, the beautiful, wide-spreading top may be butchered to make the tree fit the space. That's a shame because trimming minimizes the tree's greatest charms. Besides producing the most brilliant floral show of all Florida trees, it stands up against hurricane winds. But despite its beauty and strength, it has distinct disadvantages, such as a shallow root system that can lift sidewalks, long periods of bareness during the winter and a proclivity for dropping large seed pods and branches throughout the year. Tiny leaves also can clog pool filters and stain. The full brilliance of the plant can be enjoyed in conditions replicating its native Madagascar. They produce their best flower show on unirrigated sites. Trees under irrigation can bloom until September or October but are never as showy and are more prone to root rot.

The peltophorum, also known as the **yellow poinciana** or copperpod, can reach 70 feet or more if conditions are right. It likes a sunny, dry location and quickly produces good shade and a

161

reliable flower display. The erect clusters of golden yellow blooms are produced from May to August. These are followed by coppery-red pods that are also decorative. The deep-green compound leaves are a perfect background for the flower display. The tree is semi-evergreen, dropping leaves in the spring. It may drop all foliage if we have a freeze. This tree is also good for large properties, parks and schools where there is room for growth.

Hail to the Queen.
The **queen crape myrtle** is another spectacular summer bloomer with its foot-long panicles of bloom that range from purple through mauve to brilliant pink. It starts flowering in late May and continues until August. The tree can grow 30 to 40 feet and can be bushy unless trimmed. The large, simple leaves hold on until February and then turn red and drop off. The tree may remain bare for a month or so before new leaves emerge. A close relative is the regular crape myrtle, which is found in much of the South. A single or multistemmed small tree, it is bare for several months in winter. Large panicles in red, purple, pink, mauve or white occur in the summer. The best plants in this group have Indian tribe names and are resistant to powdery mildew, a major problem with this species..

Showers of cassias
 Cassias add beauty to the summer landscape with their big clusters of yellow or pink flowers. *Cassia fistula*, also known as golden shower, is remarkable for the long wisteria-like, drooping bunches of pale to golden yellow blooms, which can reach a foot or more in length. The yellow blooms are fragrant in the morning and can be seen in May and June. Golden shower can reach 30 feet high and sometimes shows chlorosis in the foliage in alkaline conditions. A good ixora/gardenia fertilizer applied in March, June and October will correct this problem. This cassia is an upright grower and can be useful in a narrow space. The pink shower is a wide-spreading tree with a drooping crown like a poinciana. Reaching about 20-25 feet in height and 30 feet in spread, it's deciduous in winter but produces new leaves and pink flowers from April until August. Like the poinciana, the flower show is heavier and shorter in duration if the tree is not under irrigation. All cassias need full sun and dry conditions to do their best.

Jacaranda blues

Jacaranda is a large tree that normally blooms better near Orlando than in south Florida. Its blue-purple blooms are spectacular; individual trees vary considerably in time of bloom and flower color. Some trees bloom in March but the big show comes April-June. Jacaranda normally is deciduous for one to two months in the spring before new growth and flowers appear. The trees under irrigation do not seem to lose their foliage completely, but the flower display is scattered over a longer period. Jacaranda can reach 50 to 60 feet tall in central Florida.

Q. Each year my **royal poinciana** is trimmed in October-November. The tree is pruned high up on the trunks and looks bare until it blooms in May and June. It is 35-40 feet high and 40 feet wide. What is the proper way to do the trimming?

A. A properly located poinciana with adequate growing space looks like a giant open umbrella with weeping branch ends. This growth pattern is very attractive if there is space for it. Your tree sounds like it has been "liontail" pruned — all the growth is removed except for the end of the branches, leaving a tuft of foliage resembling a lion's tail. The tree should be allowed to grow and develop properly if there is room. Poinciana has soft wood that is subject to decay, so you need to hire a good tree company to remove all the decayed or rotten wood, along with inward growing, crossing, rubbing limbs, dead wood, stubs as well as branches.

Q. I am growing a seedling of **dwarf poinciana**. It's thorny, but the poinciana I want is not thorny. Should I keep it?

A. Keep the poinciana. Dwarf seedlings are thorny, and adult trees may have few thorns on vigorous growth.

Q. My **bottlebrush has funny woody growths** all over it. The board of directors says the tree is fine and I want it replaced. What do you think?

A. I think you are right. The tree has bacterial gall, which produces woody growths throughout the tree and eventually kills it. Pruning shears that are used from one bottlebrush to another spreads the gall. Shears should be dipped in alcohol between each tree to keep them sterile. A similar bacterial gall affects oleander. Ask for a replacement tree, but stay away from bottlebrush and oleander. Few maintenance companies will dip shears in alcohol between plants, so both these plants are probably doomed if used in a condominium setting.

Q. Can you recommend **a small flowering tree that will give yellow flowers** for our front yard?
A. *Senna polyphylla* has yellow blossoms. It likes full sun and dry conditions. It normally blooms in the dry season from October to May. (March Plant of the Month)

Q. **Where can we locate a jacaranda tree?** We saw beautiful ones in St. Petersburg. We would like a 3-4 inch caliber trunk.
A. Your landscaper or retail nursery could install a 10-12 foot jacaranda for you.. Jacarandas bigger than 12 feet are difficult to find. They grow quickly although they are very open when initially planted. They quickly fill out so do not be tempted to prune them to make a denser tree.

Q. **When will my Hong Kong orchid tree bloom?**
A. Hong Kong orchid should bloom from October through March if it receives a good acid type fertilizer. Orchid trees often have chlorotic foliage if they do not receive iron and manganese. Fertilize in March, June and October. The products labeled for azaleas, gardenias and ixoras will work fine.

Q. I have a six-month old **seedling poinciana in a 5-gallon container**. The trunk is the size of a pencil, but it is 6 feet tall. **Will the trunk get heavier if I top the plant**? How do you branch this tree?
A. Plant your tree in the ground as soon as possible. Do not cut it back because it is naturally leggy when it is young and will branch out when it is three to four years old. The tree cannot survive much longer in the pot without dying back.

Q. What are your recommendations on **good small flowering trees for a 20-foot-20 foot swale?**
A. Small flowering trees would include **jatropha, yellow tabebuia, ligustrum, crape myrtle, orange jessamine standards and 'Super-King' ixora standards.**

Q. There is a tree near the ocean that has yellow flowers in the morning that change to deep red by nightfall. What is it?

A. This is the **Portia tree** (*Thespesia populnea*), a hibiscus relative. Portia trees grow well along the oceanfront and are **good for dune stabilization**. The seed capsules are somewhat prominent and make the tree look untidy. Portia tree likes sun and reaches 20-25 feet in height. A similar plant is the **mahoe**. It is big and rambling and can cover an acre or more. It is shallow and blows over easily. The flowers last only a day, then fall off. Mahoe is salt-tolerant and can tolerate beach conditions.

Q. My **frangipani** has yellow leaves. I gave it plenty of fertilizer. What should I do now?

A. Your frangipani was probably over- fertilized which caused leaf yellowing and should recover after a period of months. You might run the hose around the tree for an hour or so to flush the excess fertilizer past the roots. Frangipani do not need much water or fertilizer. They do well with little care. If you want to fertilize, use an azalea/gardenia acid fertilizer to stimulate flowers. The frangipani loses its leaves during the winter months.

Q. When should **frangipani cuttings** be planted?

A. Frangipani cuttings can be planted at anytime. Let cuttings harden off for a few days before putting them into the ground. Choose a sunny spot and allow enough room for the tree to grow to 20 feet tall and wide. The bark is very soft so plant it in a landscape bed or put liriope around the base so the weed trimmer will not girdle it.

Q. Will **a dogwood** seedling grow in South Florida?

A. Dogwood's southern limit in Florida is near Orlando.

Q. Can you give me some information about the **geiger tree**? I want a tree for the center of the front yard.

A. The tree will grow to about 25 feet tall and has orange flowers most of the year. The geiger tree has two problems. It is extremely sensitive to cold and can be frozen to the ground in severe freezes. The geiger beetle often chews holes in the leaves, which can make the tree unsightly. I would plant the tree but not as a centerpiece in the front lawn as the disadvantages are major. Use it more as a background plant where the flowers can be enjoyed but the chewed leaves would not be too obvious. The white geiger would be a better choice as it does not have bug problems and has white flowers all year. It grows to about 20 feet.

Q. The **orange geiger trees in my front yard appear to be infested**. Two years ago they had lush foliage and a cluster of healthy blooms that produced viable seeds. Now most of the new leaves turn brown and shrivel and the wood at the end of the branches looks stressed. I understand there is a beetle that infests geigers, but I cannot find any remedy. I do not want to blast the trees with chemicals.

A. Normally geigers are pretty tough trees, but they don't like damp or wet conditions. The geiger beetle infests the tree; it chews the leaves and can be controlled by Sevin. But leaves that dry and branches that die back are more serious. Check for evidence of borers – a hole with sap oozing out. If you see them, clean off the area with a cloth, poke into the hole with a wire and try to impale the borer. Then, wearing gloves, apply Dursban full strength with a paint brush. Apply 1 foot above and 1 foot below all around the trunk.

Q. Can I eat the fruit of the sausage tree?
A. **Sausage tree (*Kigelia pinnata*)** is a curiosity often found at botanical gardens, zoos and other tourist attractions. It has 3-inch claret red flowers and big green gourd-like fruit. The green seed pods get much larger and become tan or brown when the pods are ripe. They can reach 2 feet in length and are not edible. Sausage tree reaches about 30 feet in height and makes an interesting small shade tree. Sausage tree likes sun to part shade and is not a fussy plant.

Q. I want to plant an **angel trumpet tree**. What can you tell me about it?
A. I have two angel trumpet trees, a white and a peach colored form. These are large-leafed plants that do well in sun or part shade. The peach type is a much better bloomer than the white. It

cycles in and out of bloom faster and the flowers are more heavily produced. Angel trumpet trees have large leaves and are not very drought tolerant, so give them water when they start to wilt. Liquid fertilizer applied monthly between March and October hastens growth and flowering. They are subject to nematodes so grow them in an organic soil condition to repel these pests. Add 50% peat moss mixed with your existing soil to the planting hole for good results. Mulch will also repel nematodes. Keep mulch 2 inches away from the plant stems so the bark can breathe.

TREES - OTHER

Q. I lost two loquat trees near a pond. **I want to plant a mahogany tree** there now. Should I use potting soil, peat and cow manure around the tree?
A. It is usually recommended to plant mahogany in the existing soil without improving it. It's an adaptable tree and should do well. Make sure no chlorinated pond water leaks out as it can weaken or kill a tree or other plantings.

Q. Our builder planted **schefflera trees** 6 feet from our buildings. They grew as tall as the buildings in 5 years and the association had them chopped back to 5 feet, eliminating shade. Now the association wants to remove them completely. They claim the roots will damage foundations and the sprinkler systems. What do you advise?
A. I agree with the association completely. Scheffleras have extremely invasive roots that puncture and clog plumbing, lift and crack sidewalks and paving and have the potential to damage foundations. They also can start life in the tops of palms, gutters and tile roofs and drop down aerial roots to envelop the host plant and kill it. The only thing worse is ficus, which does the same damage but is bigger and can be more destructive.

Q. We planted some **strangler fig trees**, cleared away the growth around them and they are growing well. Do you have any suggestions?
A. Native strangler fig trees make good shade but have very aggressive roots that can destroy plumbing, paving and pools. I would put a barrier between the trees and whatever you wish to protect.

Q. What is **a good shade tree** to buy? I can't find any **nurseries that sell trees**.
A. Many nurseries sell trees. To find one near you, check the display ads in the Yellow Pages under "Nurseries." **Mahoganies and gumbo limbos** make good shade trees. Shade trees bring many benefits such as noise suppression, pollution reduction and lowered energy costs because of a temperature drop of 10 degrees or more under the tree on a sunny day.

Q. Can you give me the name **of a small shade tree that grows from 15 to 25 feet high**?
A. If you have an open lawn area the **carrotwood** is a good choice. It is one of our more trouble-free plants in south Florida. It makes a neat, small shade tree for smaller yards or townhouses. It is neat and doesn't drop too many leaves, but it does drop seedlings that can sprout in the landscape beds. This is more of a problem in the western mucky soil areas, especially west of State Road 7. When used on a lawn, the seedlings will be mowed before they can sprout. Carrotwood does not like a lot of water. Many of the western county areas have poor drainage. If you live in that area, I would make sure it is not planted in a low area with standing water or water that drains off slowly. Watch your watering schhedules. Remembering to water only in the mornings between 2 a.m. and 10 a.m. and only if necessary. Another good small tree is the '**Lakeview' orange jessamine**. The tree is tough with fragrant white flowers and small red fruit. It can be pruned to 15 to 20 feet. Some of the smaller palms – solitaire or tall veitchias – are also good choices.

Q. I need **a recommendation for a shade tree that does not grow more than 20-30 feet**, has a noninvasive root system and is not messy. It needs to be near the house as the property is narrow and fenced. Where could I purchase the tree?
A. A number of native plants would fit the bill, as well as some palms. The **Dahoon holly** will grow 20-30 feet and is narrow growing, so will not take up much space. It has noninvasive roots and is relatively neat. **Green buttonwood** is salt-tolerant and vertical growing in its youth. It can reach 30 feet with time. If you can't find them in stock, local retail nurseries can order both trees.

Some smaller, **narrow-growing palms** such as the **Florida thatch, solitaire, carpentaria and foxtail** will give decent shade with a narrow crown. All grow to 20-30 feet over time, with the carpentaria maxing out at 40 feet. The solitaire and thatch palms are available multi-stemmed, which can provide more shade. You can create your own clump by buying several palms of the same type at different heights and planting them together. Plant the smaller palms at an angle out from the central big vertical palm to give additional shade and add a tropical look to the landscape.

Q. My Italian pines are turning brown. What can I use to stop this condition?
A. The Italian pines are **Italian cypress**. They come from a dry climate around the Mediterranean coast which receives about 20 inches of rain a year. Our annual rainfall is 50-65 inches. The trees thrive in the dry California climate. Do not give them any water. Spray copper fungicide on the plants for Phomopsis twig blight. Follow label directions and retreat in 10 days. The only other possibility is spider mites. Spray with an insecticidal soap to control mites.

Q. **What bug is attacking my bald cypress trees at the tips**?
A. The little brown growths at the tips of your cypress trees are cones; they are perfectly natural and are the way cypress trees reproduce.

Q. Will **ginko trees** do well in South Florida?
A. We are too far south for ginkos to do well.

Q. Can you identify **my plant with the curled leaves**? What should I do to control this problem?
A. Your curly-leafed plant is a *Ficus retusa*, which should be removed because of its aggressive root system that can crack paving, plumbing and even pools. The **curled leaves are caused by thrips**. They can be controlled with a systemic insecticide such as Orthene.. The damage is just cosmetic and does not affect the tree adversely.

Q. We have a **Norfolk island pine** that is too tall and needs to come

down. If we cut it back will it still grow?
A.I would have the Norfolk Island pine cut flush with the ground.
The pine is a conifer and will not re-sprout from the stump.

Q. I have two 40-foot **Norfolk island pines** in my yard. Do the
needles cause a soil problem? I can't grow anything under them.
A. Norfolk island pines drop large amounts of needles that create a
layer that may bury small plants. Larger plantings should survive
under the pines if the lower branches are cut to 7 feet off the
ground. You might try crotons, compact jatropha, wild coffee,
firebush, or other durable plants. Remember large-leafed crotons
and wild coffee are prone to wilt and will require extra water.

Q. We have two **ficus trees** near our property line with trunk
diameters of about 2 ½ feet. They are about 45 feet from our home
on a canal. Will they cause damage to our irrigation pipes or go to
the canal for water. Should we remove some of the branches or cut
the tree down?
A. Wherever ficus roots go, they eventually cause trouble. The
South Florida Water Management District might be interested in
having them removed as a potential drainage hazard to their canals.
The trees get huge and routinely blow over . Aggressive roots can
plug plumbing, crack paving and pools, and even destroy building
slabs. I have seen roots in third floor toilets. I would opt for
removal if you can pull it off.

Q. **How do oak and other trees survive with cement or paving
all around them** and no place for water to reach them?
A. Oak and other trees with roots under paving may be reaching an
underground water source but are not getting nutrients so eventually
will decline.

Q. My **laurel oak has not had many leave**s on it for the past two
years and the **leaves that are there are spotted**. What is wrong?
A. Your laurel oak has some fungal leaf spotting. Laurel oak is
difficult to establish because many landscapers install them too
deeply in the ground. The trunk should flare out where it enters the
ground. If the trunk goes straight into the ground, it is too deep.
Trees planted too deeply cannot get enough oxygen to the roots,

and the trees die back and have few leaves. Dig down with a trowel to where the trunk flares out and remove all the excess soil from above the original root ball so the the roots can breathe. The tree should recover if it hasn't been buried too long. Spray with copper fungicide for leaf spotting.

Q. The **tree bark on my pigeon plum has started to peel** with long vertical cuts in several places. What can we do?
A Pigeon plums normally have peeling bark. If the vertical cracks are superficial I would not worry about it. Deep cracks can be caused by major tree stress like drought, excess water, etc.

Q. I was considering planting a tree in my yard like the one I saw growing on a corner of U.S.1 and SE 10th Street in Deerfield Beach. I went back later in the year and saw that it drops these big messy pods so I decided not to plant it. What kind of tree is it?
A. The tree you saw is a **bischofia** female in fruit. The fruit stains and can eat away paint. One of my clients lived in a condo and his parking space was under a female bischofia. The fruit ate away at the car's vinyl roof and ruined the paint. The adjacent condo would not cut the tree so his condo cut the tree vertically; the end result was half a tree. These trees also have invasive roots and are, as you say, messy. They often get oleander scale, which covers the leaves with white dots and causes excessive leaf drop. The seed-lings appear in flower beds and the tree has the potential to become invasive. I'm glad you don't want to plant one.

Q. I have enclosed a leaf from **a tree that just began growing in my yard**. A bird probably dropped a seed. Can you tell me what it is and if I should I keep it?
A. The leaf that you sent to me is from the **ear-leaf acacia** tree. This is a very fast growing tree that is now naturalizing in south Florida. The tree is pretty, but messy and very brittle. I would probably discard it unless you have a lot of room for a brittle tree. **Ear-leaf acacia is joining a long list of exotics that are finding Florida to their liking.** The "invaders" include the big bad three: Brazilian pepper (aka. Florida holly), casuarina and melaleuca. Newer invaders include bischofia, poinciana, woman's tongue, lead tree, *Ficus nitida*, schefflera, and many others. *

*An added note for those with access to the Internet:

- **The proliferation of exotic plants has had a profound impact on Florida's eco-system. View the EEPC List of Florida's Most Invasive Species and learn to make informed choices for your landscape that will reduce invasive plants and protect the plants that are endangered**. http:// www.fleppc.org/97list.htm

- **A**lso recommended: *Plant Invaders: How Non-native Species Invade & Degrade Natural Areas* - by John Randall on the Brooklyn Botanic Garden web site. http://www.bbg.org/ index.html

Q. Will **a Florida red maple** do well if planted where I live, which is near I-95 in West Palm Beach?

A. Florida red maple is a beautiful native tree adapted to wet areas in Florida. If the tree is planted in areas that are excessively dry, the leaves will scorch and exhibit brown areas. This is also true if the tree is located in excessively windy areas such as near the beach. I would mulch the tree with wood chips about 1-2 inches deep for moisture retention. Keep the bark about one to two inches away from the trunk so the bark can breathe. Fertilize in March, June and October with a 7-3-7 fertilizer containing manganese and iron to promote good growth.

Q. My **black olive is losing its leaves and its roots are coming up.**. We sprayed it but the leaves continue to fall. It also has a gash in the trunk. Should I put **tar** over the wound?

A. Black olive trees lose leaves usually in the spring months between March and May as the new seasons growth begins. These trees are normally quite healthy and vigorous in south Florida. Manganese problems have occurred in some areas because of high pH. A good 6-6-6- or 7-3-7 fertilizer with the minor elements of manganese and iron can be applied in March, June and October. The tree may have split or peeling bark if it is in a wet area or receiving too much water. Water the tree no more than once a week if there is no rain. Loose bark should be removed. The wound area would heal more quickly if its in the shape of a football, pointed at the top and bottom. **No tar or paint should be used on the tree.** I am curious what the tree was sprayed with. **Do not spray ran-**

domly for the sake of doing something, but only if a serious localized condition exists. Black olive roots are shallow by nature so some will appear at the surface. You could cover the root area with 1-1 ½ inches of light sandy soil and plant ground cover under the tree. Groundcover examples include artillery fern, oyster plant, Boston fern, etc. Grass will not be able to grow successfully under older black olives unless branches are lifted to let in sidelight.

Q. Our condo board has planted a **black olive** tree in our yard and its branches will be over my parking area. Will the leaves that drop off stain the white vinyl top on my car?
A. The black olive is a good shade tree, growing to 60 feet in height and 40-50 feet across. The tree is not good in parking lots as the **leaves contain tannic acid**, which can stain. This is a problem in condominiums where parking locations are permanently assigned. A permanent car cover or a new parking spot could be possible alternatives for you. Perhaps your spot could be used for guest parking.

Q. We have 30-foot **laurel oaks** at our condo that are beautiful but **we want to limit their size. Is there a growth retardant** that will help us to control the growth? The tree has too many leaves and we seem to be raking a lot.
A. Your laurel oaks are still young trees at 30 feet tall. These trees can reach 60-70 feet in height and have a spread of 50 feet or more. Laurel oak is native to South Florida and is a beautiful, generally trouble free plant, although they tend to transplant poorly. The tree is semi-deciduous, losing most of its leaves over an extended period between December and March. Growth retardant work has been researched to some degree in California, but not on laurel oak to my knowledge. Arborists and electric utility companies are very interested in growth retardants to reduce the pruning work necessary around power lines. These materials can act erratically in climates such as ours, which are very hot and humid. The University of Florida in Gainesville is working in conjunction with Chevron Corporation to develop a material to retard tree growth. The material is injected into the trunk of the tree and slows down the growth. A tall groundcover of fishtail, Boston fern, or macho fern may be useful to minimize the raking problem. The leaves sift

through the ferns to the ground and reduce the work load. Acorns probably wouldn't germinate if the fern bed is thick enough.

Q. We purchased our property because of the large **stand of pine trees**. Now someone is building a house and a pool nearby and our **trees are beginning to look like they are dying**. What is happening?
A. **Slash pines** are among the most sensitive of our native plants to any type of disturbance. Almost all slash pines near construction of any type will die within 7-10 years. Many die before that. Slash pines die from root compaction caused by heavy equipment or changes in grade or water table. Buyers of lots with slash pines often face a triple whammy. First they pay a premium for the "wooded lot", then they pay again to remove all the dying pines. They pay a third time for replacement trees. Golf courses suffer from this problem too. The slash pines cannot tolerate the daily watering they receive on many golf courses. Your best defense is to keep your pine trees healthy. Fertilize themn with a 7-3-7 fertilizer containing manganese and iron in March, June and October. Water the fertilizer in. Try half heads on your sprinkler system so the pine trees are not normally irrigated artificially except at fertilizing time.

Q. My **pigeon plum** leaves are dry and rust-colored. The tree bark has started to peel with long vertical cuts in several places. What can I do?
A. Pigeon plums normally have peeling bark. If the vertical cracks are superficial, I would not worry about it. Deep cracks can be caused by major tree stress such as drought or excess water. The leaf problem appears to be from a leaf miner. Try Orthene for control, following label directions exactly.

TREES THAT SOME PEOPLE THINK ARE PALMS, BUT AREN'T REALLY PALMS

Q. I have a **traveler's palm** as high as my screened porch. It has two shoots that are also that tall. **Can I separate the babies from the mother plant?**

A. Traveler's palms can be divided like bananas, but they make take a while to recover. Do the dividing as soon as possible. Cut off most of the upper leaves to the base of the fan; leave about four to five leaves at the top. Split the root system so each stalk will have roots. Replant immediately in an area that can accommodate a 40-foot high plant that will gradually spread out in a big space. Do not plant them under eaves or wires.

Q. How can I get **sago palm** shoots to grow?
A. Sago palm suckers can be removed from the mother plant and dipped in Rootone. Plant in a pot with well-drained potting soil. Place in the shade. The new plants should root in a few months.

Q. Can you give me any information on **the armored scale attacking sago palms**? A. This is a bad news scale. However, it is treatable with Organocide oil spray. Treat following label directions 3 times at weekly intervals. Treat the foliage above and below, the trunk and then drench the roots with the spray

Q. My **screwpine** *(Pandanus utilis)* has leaves that are bent over and half brown. What can I do to save the tree?
A. Have you done something recently that might have affected the screwpine? Weed and feed herbicide applications, over-fertilizing, weed trimmer damage, and excessive watering or mulch up against the stems and roots of the plant could all affect it negatively. Another possibility is lethal yellowing which can affect screwpine. Lethal yellowing is fatal with no realistic treatment. I would cut off the bad leaves and fertilize it lightly with palm fertilizer if it has not been fertilized to see if it makes a comeback. A spray with a fungicide like Daconil also might be useful.

TREES - PALMS

Florida's relatively flat terrain sometimes is considered boring and plantings often provide the only relief. Palms are a tropical/subtropical landscape feature that set south Florida apart from the rest of the continental United States. These signature plants range in size from small shade lovers like the 2-3 foot parlor palm to big growers like the 100-foot-plus royal palm. Foliage is distinctive, often large, and either fan or feather shaped. Try to choose self-pruning palms that drop their leaves without pruning. Avoid planting palms in open lawn areas where the weed trimmer can wound them. Try to locate palms in landscape beds away from danger of injury. The palms cannot heal wounds and are subject to fatal fungal diseases if wounded.

Q. My father has **Christmas palms**. The **fronds start turning brown**, die back and eventually only the stump is left. What is wrong?
A. **Lethal yellowing** is very common and fatal to Christmas palms. I would not buy or plant them. Along with the 'Jamaican Tall' coconut palm, they are the most susceptible. A good substitute palm with similar appearance is the solitaire or Alexander palm (same palm, two different common names.) They are similar in appearance and size to Christmas palms but are resistant to lethal yellowing. If you want a clump effect, the very similar McArthur palm is a good choice.

Q. I love the *Licuala grandis* **palm** and wonder if it will grow **in a shady spot on the west side** of the house. It is sunny there from June to September. If it does not work there, is there a similar palm that will work?
A. The *Licuala grandis* is a unique understory rain forest palm that needs shade. It is also quite cold sensitive. I would make every effort to incorporate it into your landscape if you can find year-round shade and shelter from cold winds. There is nothing else with a round, undivided leaf like this palm. Consider moving something less valuable out of the way to accommodate it.

Q. Our two **coconut palms** look like they have **crown rot**. Can this be prevented?
A. Spray the buds of the coconuts with Daconil to prevent bud rot. Follow directions and repeat treatment as necessary.

Q. I want to plant a **coconut tree** in my yard. **Do we still have to worry about lethal yellowing**?
A. Lethal yellowing never went away but did decrease in activity

for a number of years. Malayan Dwarf coconuts are highly resistant to lethal yellowing (95%), but have straight stems and do not have the vigor of the 'Jamaican Tall' coconut. They require fertilizing in March and October with a good palm fertilizer high in boron to maintain vigor. The green form is the most vigorous type available of the Malayan Dwarf varieties. The Maypan coconut is a hybrid with about 90% resistance to lethal yellowing. It has similar vigor and appearance to the 'Jamaican Tall' variety and is better than the Malayan Dwarf types for the oceanfront. Tetracycline injections can still be used on the 'Jamaican Tall' types, but must be redone every three months.

Q. I **planted some coconut seeds** from resistant varieties. How long must I wait until they sprout?
A. Sprouting coconuts from seed may not be a good idea because of the active presence of lethal yellowing. The coconuts you collect will probably not have high resistance because they have been cross-pollinated by bees and other insects. You will know the characteristics of the parent coconut, but not know what other coconuts the bees had been visiting. Some coconuts will sprout within a few months and others take longer. Give the coconuts about a year to germinate before throwing them out.

Q I recently planted a **Madagascar palm** and now the **leaves are falling off**. What is wrong?
A. Your palm leaves have scale, which is causing the leaves to drop. Use a systemic insecticide such as Dexol houseplant systemic for control of scale and mealybug. Repeat treatment in 10 days to kill hatching eggs.

Q. I had a five-stemmed **pygmy date palm**, which now only has three stems. The new **leaves look grayish-white** on the surface. What's wrong?
A. It probably has **frizzletop**, which can kill the palm. It's a manganese deficiency. I have seen this on **royal palms, paurotis palm, pygmy date palm and queen palm** most frequently. Fertilize the palm in March, June and October with palm fertilizer containing manganese. Get manganese sulfate immediately and sprinkle around the palm over the whole area that the leaves cover

as well as a foot beyond. Use about ¼ to 1 pound on pygmy date palms, depending on plant size. The tree should recover and make new healthy growth. The manganese treatment should be done every June from now on.

Q. Our condo association wants to plant **queen palms**. What do you think?
A. Although queen palms are nice looking I consider them overplanted in south Florida. Many condos and commercial properties do not maintain their plantings and you see queen palms in decline or dead all through these projects. Queen palms need an application of a good palm fertilizer in March, June, and October as well as an annual treatment of manganese sulfate of about one pound for every 10 feet of plant height or else death is the result.

Q. We have three **queen palms**. Two have **fungal bracts** growing on the bottom of the trunks. Can we eradicate this without harming the plants?
A. Palms cannot heal wounds or any injury by mower, string trimmer, etc. These injuries provide entry points for various fungal and insect problems. Queen palms are very subject to fatal and incurable Ganoderma butt rot, which enters through wounds near the soil. Fungal bracts on the trunk would indicate the butt rot is active. The palms would last about three to four years and dies. Do not plant any other palms in the area; they will die, too. Replace the palms with a regular tree or shrub.

Q. My a**reca palm keeps losing leaves** even though new ones appear. Some **leaves are flecked**. Is it dying?
A. Unfortunately the natural life of areca palm includes fairly constant shedding. The palm produces a new leaf at the top as an old leaf dies off further down the stem. Areca palms are clump-type growers with many stems, so the leaf or frond dropping is a fairly continuous business. It slows in the winter as the palm grows more slowly. If some stems died I would be suspicious of Ganderma butt rot. This is a fairly common problem on areca and queen palms if they are in a poorly draining area or are receiving excess water from the sprinkler. You may see shelf-like mushroom bracts at the base of the palm. Keep your palm on the dry side – water no more

than two times a week, ½ hour per zone, in the morning only. I usually follow nature and set the sprinkler on manual for the wet season (June through October) and on automatic for the dry season (November through May). Acreca palms should be fertilized in March, June, and October with a good palm fertilizer to encourage vigor. Off-color flecked leaves on areca are from a potassium deficiency. Make sure your fertilizer analysis is high in potassium, the last number of the three main elements.

Q. Our association wants to plant **royal palms.** Are they hard to grow? How long do they take to get big?
A. Royal palms are not hard to grow and they increase in size quite quickly. Be careful where you site them because of the big leaves, 15 to 20 feet long weighing up to 80 pounds, and the huge size of the mature palm, 70 to 100 feet tall. Be sure to keep the trees away from overhead wires. Commercial nurseries and Palm Society sales would probably be the best source on royal palms. Your local retail nursery can order for you.

Q. How **can we cut off the burlap-like material on coconut palms**? **Is there a special way to cut off the leaves**? How do we keep the large **red ants** from nesting in the burlap material?

A. Cut frond stems off flush with the trunk, but do not cut them above the 10-2 o'clock position on the tree. The 9-3 o'clock position is even better. The tree needs green leaves to make energy for growth. Radical pruning can weaken or kill the palm. The burlap-like material forms at the leaf bases and falls off naturally as the leaves drop off. It can never be removed, as it is part of the plant. You can spray the burlap material with Dursban, which will kill the ants. They may re-nest there in the future but as the tree grows taller the ants will be less of a problem.

Q. Can you tell me what is wrong with my palms? The landscaper says they are fine. I can't stand looking at them
A. Nothing is wrong with the palms. They are young "**booted**" **cabbage palms** that are the state tree of Florida. The boots are old leaf bases that remain after the leaves are cut off. As the palm gets older the boots fall off leaving a smooth trunk. Ferns and oyster

plants are growing in the boots, which is normal and does no harm. If ficus or schefflera start growing in the boots the palm can eventually become strangled and killed. You could have the boots cut off by a good arborist if you desire. "Booted" palms are considered desirable and usually cost more than the smooth older trees but beauty is in the eyes of the beholder. You are definitely not in Kansas anymore from a horticultural standpoint

Q. My **Bismarkia palm** has new fronds that are not opening properly. What do you think is causing this?
A. Bismarkia palms normally are quite trouble-free. They sometimes have fused leaves if nutrition is a problem. DeArmand Hull, a palm specialist in Dade County advises that manganese deficiency can affect Bismarkias. Fertilize in March, June and October with palm fertilizer and treat yearly with manganese sulphate. Apply manganese sulphate right away.

VEGETABLES and some Special Edibles

Q. I have some **spots on my green pepper leaves**. Will they affect pepper yields? What control do you recommend?
A. Your pepper leaves have some fungal spots. Water in the morning only and keep water off the foliage. Try copper fungicide for control.
Q. I have a garden box with **tomatoes** that are planted in a mixture of topsoil and cow manure. The green plants are lush but have few flowers or fruit. The fruit are small. What do you recommend?
A. You may have a soil too rich in nitrogen that is promoting leafy growth instead of flowers and fruit. To promote more flowering, use a generic "bloom special" liquid fertilizer. If bees are scarce, cross-pollinate with an artist's paintbrush by brushing each flower center with the bristles. This will help to set the fruit. The season for tomatoes begins in October and winds down in late April or May. Cherry tomatoes can continue through the summer months.

Q. I have **whitefliy and blossom-end rot on my tomatoes**. I used a malathion/Sevin spray for whitefly. What can I do for control?

180

A. A calcium treatment would take care of the blossom-end rot. The malathion/Sevin spray you used on the whitefly probably killed the pollinating bees. In the future, try yellow sticky boards for the whitefly. Put a board on a post and paint it with cadmium yellow paint. Cover the painted board with a light gear oil. Whitefly is attracted to the yellow board and will stick to the oil and die. Wipe off the oil and repeat as needed. Good lizards can stick to the board, so be careful.

Q. My **tomato plants have started to wilt**. I have grown tomatoes for years and feed them with 10-12-8 tomato food. Some plants start to wilt when the fruit is 2-3 inches in size. Why?
A. Your tomatoes probably have fusarium or verticillium wilt. **Select VFN resistant tomato varieties** in the future. Keep water off the leaves and keep the plant drier. Use a copper fungicide spray on the plant, which may offer some help. Rotate your tomato plants and do not put them in the same place each year. Try growing them in 5-gallon buckets instead.

Q. My climbing **tomatoes are splitting and the leaves are brown and dry** even though I water every day. Why?
A. You probably watered them too much. Excess water also ruins the flavor and causes fertilizer to leach past plant roots before the plants can use it. Brown leaves are symptomatic of various fungal and root rot diseases. Water your plants in the morning only once every three to four days after they are established.

Q. My tomato plants have **white wiggle marks in the leaves**. What are they?
A. You have leaf miners, which are more of a nuisance that anything else. They do not affect the fruit and only make the leaves unsightly. Leaf miners are small caterpillars that burrow in between the leaf layers so they can't be reached with a regular insecticide. A systemic product would do them in, but also will affect the fruit to some degree. I would leave them alone and enjoy your tomatoes. Your tomato plants can have as much as 60% of its foliage affected with leaf miner and the fruit will not suffer. If you do not have too many infected leaves you can pinch them off.

Q. My **tomatoes** are growing and blooming well but **no fruit.** We do not seem to have pollinating insects. **How do I hand pollinate**?
A. Buy an artists paintbrush and put the brush into each flower to transfer pollen from one bloom to another. You are playing bee and the pollinated flowers should produce fruit.

Q. My cabbage leaves, peppers, tomatoes **all have bites in them**. What can I do to correct the problem?
A. Your leaves are being chewed by a caterpillar and worms are attacking the tomatoes. Use Dipel, a safe organic pesticide for caterpillars. Follow label instructions for application and repeat spray seven to ten days later. Harvest tomatoes early when they are just starting to turn red to minimize worm damage. Keep foliage dry, using a soaker hose and water in the morning only to minimize fungal leaf spots.

Q. My **lettuce is limp and light green** even though it gets plenty of sun. Why?
A. Lettuce is a cool weather crop that can be sown between September and January. Limp pale lettuce could be attributed to growing the plants in the full sun. A cooler location with morning sun only would result in better quality lettuce.

Q. Where can I get the **romaine lettuce** seed that commercial growers use? The plants I get from regular seed companies look like weeds.
A. 'Jericho' is a heat-tolerant romaine lettuce. Bred in Israel, it has large heavy heads that are nicely shaped and very crunchy. It should be planted anytime between September and January and can be harvested 60 days later. If the soil is above 80 degrees, the seed will stay dormant until the weather cools. Be sure to keep the soil cool at germination time. Jericho is available through Shepard's Garden Seeds.

Q. I want to plant **watermelon**. When will I know when it is ripe?
A. Watermelon is ripe usually 80-100 days after planting. They are planted in February and March so should be ripe by July. When you tap the end of the watermelon it should sound hollow.

Q. I planted **corn** in my yard but the ears are small and malformed.

What causes this to happen?

A. Soil sterilization is an important necessity in South Florida with vegetable gardens because of nematodes and soil-borne disease. Plant selection is very important. The corn may also be suffering from poor cross-pollination. You need to plant a good amount of corn in a square or rectangle for good pollination and ear formation. Corn is pollinated by the wind. I suspect you may have some nutritional problems as well.

Q. I am losing my **zucchini** to rot. What is wrong?

A. Spray the plants with copper fungicide and repeat treatment in 10 days.

Q. Can **vegetable cuttings, seeds and small plants be planted in straight compost**? Does the compost need topsoil added?

A. New vegetable plants/seeds/cuttings can be started in mid-September if they are protected from heavy rains. They are usually set out in the garden in mid-October when the dry season normally starts. Add one-third perlite or vermiculite to the compost for good aeration and stability. Give the plants as much sun as possible after they are hardened off to get the best results.

Q. What are the most common **strawberry** varieties grown in South Florida?

A. The most common strawberries grown here include Florida 90, Tioga, Florida belle, Douglas and Sequoia.

Q. Our **cucumbers and squash** bloom well but do not set fruit. We used fruit set spray to no avail.

A. I would suspect a lack of pollinating insects like bees. Avoid spraying which could kill the bees. If you must spray do it at dusk when the bees are not pollinating. You could play bee and transfer pollen from flower to flower with the tip of an artist's paintbrush

Q. What can I do to control caterpillars on my **bush beans**? I want an organic product safe for my family.

A. Use Thuricide or Dipel, which are organic stomach poisons that only affect caterpillars. Follow label directions exactly.

Q. I grow tomatoes every year on my screened porch but must fight off **a plague of whitefly**. Where do they come from and what can I do to control them?

A. Check your plants very carefully to make sure they do not have whitefly when you buy them. An extra strong pyrethrum spray will control the whitefly and is organic.

Q. Is it better to use last year's **soil in planting flowers and vegetables** in pots or to use fresh soil?

A. Many people use the prior year's soil with success but ideally I would use new soil.

Q. What **vegetables can I grow on my condo porch**? I am from New York. What is the season here?

A. You can grow vegetables between October and May. Tomatoes and peppers are the usual container favorites but herbs and others are also suitable. Five- gallon paint buckets with holes punched in them for drainage are best for tomatoes.

VINES

I consider vines a mixed bag. Many vines grow so big they quickly overwhelm the flimsy trellises they may grow on. Our long growing season promotes supervines so you must research carefully before introducing them to your property. Some are extremely aggressive. I constantly battle moonvine, which is a pretty native with white morning glory-like blooms that open at night. This vine is sold in seed packets as an annual up north. Here it eats telephone poles for breakfast. This and the similar air potato grow from tubers so are hard to eradicate. Many other aggressive vines lurk out there like kudzu, sewer vine, Gold Coast jasmine, etc.

The beauty of blooming vines cannot be denied and some produce flower displays unrivaled in the plant kingdom. They are useful for narrow areas creating a vertical garden and covering unsightly chain link fences sheds and other bad views. They also provide food, nesting sites and cover for many birds and small animals.

Vines grow in different ways and provisions should be made for how they grow. The **twiners** twist around a trellis or stem as they progress up their support. This growth habit is good for fences and trellises if you do not have to paint or maintain them. The vines cannot be untwisted when maintenance time comes. These vines are lethal if growing up a tree or other living support. The twining growth does not permit the trunks of the host plant to expand naturally and they gradually strangle the host plant. Examples include honeysuckle, queen's wreath (*Petrea volubilis),* wisteria, jasmine, confederate jasmine and Carolina jessamine.

Scrambling vines are usually leaning types such as allamanda, plumbago, etc. These are among the easiest vines to control and usually do not get excessively large.

Clinging vines include ivy, Virginia creeper, trumpet vine, pothos, scindapsus, chalice vine and others with rootlets that cling to the surface and support the vine as it clings. These vines are especially effective on large bare cement walls. They should not be used on wood shingles, fences or on houses generally. The clinging vines adhere tightly to their support and provide good habitat for insects such as termites, ants and spiders, and other wildlife. The tight growth promotes decay through poor air circulation and dampness. Other vines climb by **tendrils** like grape or by thorns like bougainvillea and roses.

Vines can create an enormous amount of work if they are not carefully chosen. Smaller, easily controlled vines like allamanda, small bougainvilleas, confederate jasmine, Carolina jessamine, bleeding heart vine, etc. are preferred to some of the available giants. Remember that most vines and other plants bloom at the ends of their branches. Hacked back bougainvillea will result in a big thorny mess.

If you haven't guessed by now, I am the ultimate lazy gardener and M.E. DePalma is an incurable romantic so it isn't surprising that when it comes to vines we disagree. M.E. insisted that she be able to plead the following paragraph:

You might consider installing a garden arch, like those found in French gardens. Use it as a pass way to your garden. Let the vines cling to it and in that way they are away from your walls. If you want to attract butterflies and hummingbirds, you'll want to add some vines. Passion vine is a larval food source for several species of butterfly including the Zebra, Julia and Gulf frittilary.

Aristolochia vine is the food source for the Pipevine and Polydamus Swallowtail. Clitoria is a wonderful vine with woody stalk. The vine produces the richest cobalt blue flowers you have ever seen! It is a delightful burst of color along a fence. It has small leaves and is not messy or thorny like bougainvillea. Blue sky (*Thunbergia grandiflora)* can be aggressive...like coming in the dog door. But in the right location it can be magnificent. One friend uses it over an arbor to form the archway leading to the canal. Sure, she has to hack it back each year but so what…it is worth it!

Q. My **bougainvillea** has flowers but **no leaves**. It has been this way for 18 months. I fertilize and water. What can I do?
A. Fertilize in March, June and October with an acid type ixora/azalea/gardenia fertilizer for best results. Bougainvilleas sometimes have difficulty if the drainage is not perfect. Some of the inland communities have poor drainage, and plants have difficulty getting established or get root rot. Think about where you put it. Bougainvilleas are thorny and grow huge—some reaching more than three stories in height. Give the plant plenty of room to grow well.

Q. My **bougainvillea** is growing but it **has no blossoms**. Why?
A. Bougainvillea normally bloom best in the winter dry season between November and May. The summer wet season is usually a time of growth. The old fashioned purple bougainvillea (*glabra*) often blooms year round. Bougainvilleas need full sun and dry conditions to perform well. They perform beautifully in the semi-arid regions of Arizona and California and in the Florida Keys where water is so expensive. I would keep your bougainvillea totally dry and dependent solely on rainfall if it is in the ground. Fertilize with a good azalea/gardenia fertilizer to encourage bloom in March, June and October.

Q. Something is **chewing the leaves** on my **bougainvillea** vine?
A. Use Dipel for caterpillar control. Beetles and weevils can be contolled by spraying with liquid Sevin in the late evening. Repeat spraying in 7 to 10 days following label directions. Leaf miners leave serpentine trails on the foliage and may be controlled with Orthene.

186

Q. Can I put **bougainvillea in a pot** in full sun on my **condo patio** if I water it daily?
A. Bougainvillea does best if it is kept somewhat dry. Unglazed clay pots are good containers for bougainvillea as they breathe and disperse excess water quickly. Plastic pots are all right but need to be watched because of slow drainage. The soil should be dry to the touch when you water to the depth of your forefinger. When you water put enough in so water drains out the bottom of the pot. If you have saucers beneath the pots use a meat baster to siphon excess water off. Many apartments and condos have rules about water dripping off your balcony. Water early in the morning or late at night to avoid conflict with neighbors below. Keep foliage dry if you water in the evening to avoid fungal problems. Fertilize monthly between March and October with Peters 20-20-20 for good blooms.

Q. What **vine will cling** to the posts of my porch and bloom most of the year?
A. Vines that cling and bloom are rare in Florida. Most need to be woven through a trellis for support. Clinging vines climb by little holdfasts (small little roots that attach to what it is climbing on). The clinging vines are also woody and will get large. They include the trumpet vine, a native mostly summer blooming plant. It is found in the northern part of the state but will grow here. The hybrid, 'Mme.Galen', is considered the best because it does not sucker or seed. The flowers attract hummingbirds and butterflies.

Another big clinging vine is the cup-of-gold (*Solandra maxima*), which has large gold cup-like blooms. It has a coconut fragrance at night and blooms most of the year. The plants contain an atropine-like sap, which is poisonous and causes hallucinations.

Two non-blooming clinging vines are Virginia creeper and *Ficus repens*, which are also big growers. The clinging vines would be all right on concrete, as the aerial roots would dig right into the concrete. Wood would not be a good surface because of the rot and decay in this climate. These vines would be of very limited availability, but your nurseryman should be able to order them for you.

Q. I have a **bleeding heart vine** and want to give some to my friends. When is **the best time to take cuttings**?

A. Bleeding heart blooms a good part of the year and is quite trouble free. Try giving out rooted cuttings from April through July. You should have good success then.

Q. Would **passion vine** growing over Bermuda roof tiles hurt the roof? They would be an improvement over the mildewed tiles.

A. I am leery of any vine growing over a roof. The passion vine is fast growing and could get under the tiles. The vines could cause the wood beneath the tiles to rot through, admitting excess moisture and providing a haven for insects like carpenter ants.

Q. Can I grow **kiwi** here?

A. Kiwi is a vine that does well in north Florida, the lower south and the west coast states. It is a vigorous twining vine that must have a strong support. Kiwi vines can reach 30 feet or more in size. The plants need a male and female present to insure good pollination and fruit production.

Q. I have an old a**llamanda** vine that has stopped blooming. What can I do to get it to bloom again?

A. Allamanda blooms on new wood. You probably removed a lot of this when you pruned your plant. I would leave it alone unless it is growing over a sidewalk, or otherwise getting in your way. Fertilize in March, June and October with azalea-gardenia acid fertilizer. Allamanda needs full sun for heaviest flower production.

Q. I planted a **wood rose** vine six months ago; it is growing fast but it still hasn't flowered.

A. Wood rose is a fast growing, tuberous rooted climbing vine, which can take over the neighborhood if you are not careful. I rank this with kudzu, moonvine and air potato as a real pest. It is in the morning glory family and has yellow flowers which are quite pretty. The "wood rose" is actually the fruit structure which usually sets after bloom. Your plant may not be old enough to set fruit properly. Wood rose does too well in south Florida and needs only a good amount of sun to bloom well. Prune it as needed to keep it from overrunning treetops and smothering them.

Q. An **orange-stemmed vine** is choking my impatiens. What can I do?

A. You have orange–stemmed dodder or love vine. A true parasite, it can grow on plant stems and roots. Remove all of it before it seeds. It will not react to herbicides because it has no chlorophyll. The only way to get rid of it is by hand pulling. If it is growing on a plant stem or root it needs to be cut off.

Q. What vines can I plant that **bear edible fruit?**

A. Chayote is a tropical vine bearing edible fruit. It is very popular in the Latin American countries and is used like a squash in cooking. Some varieties of passion vine are also edible.

Q. I have orange **colored caterpillars on my yellow mandevilla** vine. What can I do to control them?

A. Dipel or Thuricide are organic controls for caterpillars. The caterpillars will not be eliminated completely and may come back in future months. They feed for a short time and then become butterflies which are pretty in the garden. I would give up a few leaves for the butterflies.

MISCELLANEOUS QUESTIONS ????

Q. We are new arrivals to South Florida and are overwhelmed at the variety of plants and things to learn. Can you **recommend some places to go or books to read?**

A. New arrivals to Florida can be bewildered by the vast array of exotic plants and new things to learn. The first place I would go to is the **Mounts Horticultural Learning Center.** This small botanical garden in West Palm Beach is perfect for the newcomer as plantings are grouped by usage. Examples include hedge plantings, native plants, flowering trees, salt-tolerant plants, herbs, tropical fruit trees, etc. Most of the plants are labeled. Bring a pad along to write down the names of your favorites. The garden is located directly behind the Palm Beach Co-operative Extension Office. All **Extension Offices** are wonderful resources on gardening questions. They have plant clinics for specific plant problems and excellent free literature on a wide range of gardening topics and recipes if you become a tropical fruit enthusiast.

There is a series of small books by Lewis Maxwell at a cost of around $6 each that has a lot of good basic information. These include subjects such as Florida vegetables, fruits, insects, flowers, trees, lawns and gardens. Write to him for more information (see suppliers list).

The state of Florida puts out two excellent books free to Florida residents. One is *Flowers, Shrubs, and Trees for Florida Homes* and the other is *Native Trees and Plants for Florida Landscaping.* Write Florida Department of Agriculture and Consumer Services for these books.

I think the best horticultural bookstore is at **Fairchild Gardens** in Coral Gables. This is well worth a field trip, and the gardens are beautiful. **Flamingo Gardens** in Fort Lauderdale is also a good horticultural spot to visit and has a nice plant shop with some rare plants available. **Nova University has a medicinal garden** where you can see the plants and read about their pharmaceutical properties.

Educational classes are held at all of the gardens and at the Extension offices. If you feel like getting more involved, there are garden clubs galore. There are specialty clubs on orchids, begonias, cacti and succulents, bonsai, rare fruit and vegetables, hibiscus, gesneriads, roses, aeroids, native plants, etc.

Broward Community College offers a complete two -year horticultural degree at its main campus in Davie. This is an excellent high quality program. Various adult education programs also offer gardening classes from time to time. Garden clubs offer horticultural lessons at every meeting and many are open to the public.

Q. Enclosed is the soil from **the flower box attached to my villa**. The impatiens wilt and die when they are planted in the box. I have the same plants in a plastic flower box and they are doing fine. What do you suggest?
A. Your soil is probably infected with Rhizoctonia disease. Subdue may offer some control. Follow label directions and treat the soil.

The planter boxes attached to buildings are usually a nightmare in one way or another. They are usually under building eaves, so must be watered by hand or with an irrigation system. The boxes often leak into the house. Bug populations quickly build up under the eaves, particularly spider mites. Plants usually suffer one way or another. I personally would cover the soil in the box with a weed barrier and put decorative red lava rock or river rock over the weed barrier.

Q. You write about **invasive plants** and suggest removing most of them from the yard. But, some of Florida's weeds are attractive. My tradescantia was given to me by a neighbor a two years ago. There were a few sprigs and I tossed them at the bottom of a ficus tree. Other weeds like oyster plant and mother-in-law's tongue have their place in the landscape as well.
A. You are correct. Such plants can be used if you select the proper place that controls their invasive habit. I recently used mother-in-law's tongue against a wall in a narrow bed along a sidewalk. It is limited by the concrete and cannot spread to other parts of the yard. It is a perfect location for this aggressive plant. Ficus roots are a horror and the tradescantia covers them nicely. As the roots expand and the grass dies off the tradescantia will continue to cover the bare ground so it will not be too noticeable. Common sense is the key to good planting and pest control!

Recommended websites:
The Florida Wild Flower Showcase at
http://www.flwildflowers.com

FLORIDA WEATHER

Florida's weather is marked by a pronounced winter dry season and a summer wet season. The dry season usually begins in mid-October and ends at the end of May. The wet season lasts from early June to mid-October. The dry season can really be dry with April and May causing great stress to plantings. New growth is in full swing with no rainfall to prevent wilting and dieback. These two months are the most critical for supplementary watering. The summer wet season coincides with the hurricane season, when these tropical systems bring some of the rainy weather.

Annual rainfall averages 50-65 inches over the southern peninsula. Inland areas typically receive 10-15 inches more rainfall than coastal areas. Storms build up over the central part of the state and generally move west toward the Gulf coast. The summer wind pattern is generally east to west while winter wind patterns are west to east. We are under tropical influences during the summer and temperate conditions in the winter.

Freezes are not common in south Florida but can occur in any year. The Keys are frost free. Frost/freeze damage is possible between December and mid-March. If a freeze is expected pull mulch away from plantings and water thoroughly the night the cold front is expected. The soil will release heat in the air and can create a warm area near the plants. Bring tender potted plants inside. Cover tender outside plants with a sheet or light blanket. Do not use plastic to cover plants.

Water has a warming effect and can protect plants from freezing. The southeast coast of Lake Okeechobee is noticeably warmer than other parts of the lakes shore. In Broward county and other areas on the southeast coast the gulf stream has a noticeable warming effect. Be careful when using tropical plants inland as they can be frozen or killed by freezes or frosts.

One basic thing to remember is that spring is fall and fall is spring. We plant vegetables and annuals in October and they finish off in April-May. Evergreen leaves fall off in the spring which is leaf raking time.

SOIL

Soil types vary but generally soils are alkaline with some acid pockets as one progresses northward in the state. Coastal soils are generally sandy with organic muck type soils in central parts of the state. Some coastal areas have marl soils which are similar to clay soils up north and have excellent moisture retention. The Redlands in Dade County also have properties similar to clay. South Dade county has rock soils which are almost impossible to plant directly in. Planting holes need to be augered in. Many gardeners used raised beds in these areas.

SPECIAL PLACES & SUPPLIERS LIST

Arbico Environmentals, P.O. Box 4247, Tucson AZ., 85738-1247 (800-827-2847)
Arbor Grow: in Fort Lauderdale - Organic Insecticides, (954-583-8634)

The **Bug Store** 113 West Argonne Street in St. Louis, Mo. 63122-1104. (800-455-2847)

Extension Service Offices have recipes for both green and ripe mangoes. In Broward County, 3245 College Avenue, Davie, 33314, (954-370-3725). In Palm Beach County, (561-276-1260 and 683-1777) and in Dade County, (305-248-3311)
The **Division of Plant Industry** has regional numbers. Inspection agents are usually at the phone from 8-8:30 a.m. and from 4-4:30 p.m.; at other times, leave a recorded message. Call (352-372-3505) in **Gainesville** for inspection forms, etc.

Fairchild Tropical Gardens, 10901 Old Cutler Road, Miami, (305-667-1651)
Flamingo Gardens, 3750 Flamingo Road, Fort Lauderdale (954-473-2955)
Florida Department of Agriculture and Consumer Services, Mayo Building room 115, Tallahassee, FL.32304

Iowa Pyro Supply, 1000 130th St., Stanwood, Iowa, 52337, (319-945-6637)

Lewis Maxwell, 6230 Travis Blvd., Tampa, FL 33610 *Florida Poisonous Plants, Snakes, and Insects* around $5.oo, plus shipping also various garden books at around $6.00 plus S&H.
Mounts Horticultural Learning Center, 531 North Military Trail, West Palm Beach, (561-683-1777)

George W. Park Seed, Cokesbury Road, Greenwood, S.C. (864-223-7333)
Park's Seed, 1 Parkton Ave., Greenwood, SC 29647-0001. (800-845-3369

- **Pond Plants**
  - **Lily Pons Water Gardens**, P.O. Box 10, Lilly Pons, MD. 21712-0010
  - **Slocum Water Gardens,** 1101 Cypress Gardens Rd., Winter Haven, FL 33880
  - **Tropical Pond & Garden** 17888 61Place North, Loxahatchee, FL 33470 (561-791-8994)
  - **Aquatic Plant Management** in Plantation (954-462-0868) sells and installs spike rush.

Safer Gardens, P.O. Box 1665, New York, NY 10116
Shepard's Garden Seeds, 6116 Highway 9, Felton, CA. (408-335-6910)

Books: Many major bookstore chains carry South Florida gardening books, but the greatest variety can be found from garden specialty sources. They include:
Bookstores in the various Botanical Gardens listed on the Internet connection page
Mail order houses such as **Arborist Supply House** (954-561-9527) and **Betrock Information Services**, 7770 Davie Road Extension, Hollywood (in Broward, call 954-981-2821; all others call 800-561-3819).

For plant identification try
Betrock's Florida Plant Guide (Betrock) by Edward F. Gilman
Betrock's Reference Guide to Florida Landscape Plants (Betrock) by Timothy K. Broschat and Alan W. Meerow
Florida, My Eden (Florida Classics Library) by Frederic B. Stresau Sr.
Florida Gardener's Guide (Cool Springs Press) by Tom MacCubbin and Georgia Tasker

Native Florida Plants (Gulf Publishing) by Robert Haehle and Joan Brookwell
Tropicals by Gordon Courtright
Gardens by the Sea (University Press) by: The Garden Club of Palm Beach

For plant care try
Tropical Gardening (Pantheon Books) by David Bar-Zvi
The Art of South Florida Gardening (Pineapple Press) by Harold Songdahl and Coralee Leon

Other books
The Tropical Look (Timber Press) with photographs by South Florida plant experts, including Larry Schokman and Roger Hammer
The Gardener's Computer Companion: Hundreds of Easy Ways to Use Your Computer for Gardening (No Starch Press), by Bob Boufford
The New Western Gardening Book available through Sunset Books, Lane Publishing Co., Mcnlo, CA., 94025
The Gardens of Florida (Pelican) By Steven Brooke and Laura Cerwinske
Florida Butterfly Gardening (University Press of Florida) By Marc C. Minno and Maria Minno

OTHER SOURCES OF INFORMATION

STARTING OUT ONLINE

The Weather Channel **http://www.weather.com**
Florida Gardener **http://www.floridagardener.com/**
Florida Plants Online **http://www.floridaplants.com/**
Hortworld **http://www.hortworld.com**/
Garden Bed **http://www.gardenbed.com**
Virtual Garden **http://vg.com/**
garden.com **http://www.garden.com**
The Garden Web at **http://www.gardenweb.com/**
John Doyle's photos of over 100 plants that will thrive in south Florida is at **http://gardenfla.com/**

FAIRS, which stands for Florida Agricultural Information Retrieval System, has been one of the Top 5 Southern Gardening links since the beginning. **http://edis.ifas.ufl.edu/**

SITES THAT WILL ANSWER YOUR QUESTIONS

Do you know what wildlife species are in danger of extinction in your county? The Florida Extension Service **http://www.wec.ufl.edu/ Extension/** has that information and a lot more including the steps to take for creating a wildlife habitat in your backyard.

If you ever wondered what wildflower was blooming in that vacant lot check out the photos at Florida Wildflower Showcase **http:// www.flwildflowers.com/** and you'll learn to call it by name.

If you'd like to join a garden club visit The Florida Federation of Garden Clubs
at **http://www.ffgc.org**
Locate what clubs are available in your district, take virtual tours of members gardens, learn about floral design, and youth camp, apply for a scholarship and find out what shows, classes and tours are coming to your area. You can also get directions to the *Nova Medicinal Garden*. The garden is a great place to learn about South Florida plants with medicinal properties. You will also find links to many of the sites mentioned in this book along with links that will take you on tours of other Great Florida Gardens.

DIGGING DEEP

Butterflies for Dade County **http://www.npwrc.usgs.gov/resource/ distr/lepid/bflyusa/chklist/states/counties/fl_25.htm** All the counties in Florida have lists at this site but finding them without the county number just isn't that easy. An index of Butterflies of Florida by County is at **http://159.189.96.215/resource/distr/lepid/bflyusa/chklist/states/ fl.htm** Once you find a site like that, Bookmark it!

Plants

The Celebrating Wildflowers Coloring Book –the scientific and common names of Native Plants
http://www.aqd.nps.gov/npci/color/index.htm

The Florida Wildflower pages **http://www.flwildflowers.com**
University of Florida Herbarium (FLAS)
http://www.flmnh.ufl.edu/natsci/herbarium

ISB: Atlas of Florida Vascular Plants – Maps
http://www.usf.edu/~isb/projects/atlas/dic-bc.html

Florida Plants Online
http://www.floridaplants.com/homepage.html

United States Department of Agriculture: PLANTS National Data Base
http://plants.usda.gov/plants/

Florida Exotic Pest Plant Council **http://www.fleppc.org**
The Florida Center for Environmental Studies:
http://www.ces.fau.edu/

Aquatic Plants

U.S. Army Corps of Engineers Aquatic Plant Control:
http://www.saj.usace.army.mil/conops/apc/apc_page.html

Places to Visit

Fairchild Tropical Gardens **http://www.ftg.org**
The Wildlife Care Center **http://www.wildcare.org**

State Parks and Botanical Gardens

Big Pine Key
   Bahia Honda State Park
   36850 Overseas Hwy Big Pine Key, 33043 305-872-2353

Fort Lauderdale Area
   Bonnet House **http://www.bonnethouse.com**
   900 N Birch Road, Ft. Lauderdale, 33304 954-563-5393

   Butterfly World **http://www.butterflyworld.com**
   3600 S Sample Road, Coconut Creek, 33073 305-977-4400

   Flamingo Gardens and Arboretum
   3750 S. Flamingo Road, Davie, 33330-1698 305-473-2955

   The Morikami Museum of Japanese Culture
   http://www.icsi.com/ics/morikami/
   4000 Morikami Park Road, Delray Beach, 33446-2305

407-495-0233

Fort Pierce Area
   Heathcote Botanical Gardens
   210 Savannah Road, Fort Pierce, 34982-3447
   407-464-4672

   McKee Botanical Gardens
   East side of South US1, Vero Beach,   407-234-1949

Homestead
   Biscayne National Park **http://www.nps.gov/bisc/**
   PO BOX 1369, Homestead, 33090   305-230-1100

   Everglades National Park **http://www.nps.gov/ever/**
   P.O. Box 279, Homestead, 33030   305-247-6211

   Fruit and Spice Park
   24801 SW 187th Avenue, Homestead, FL 33031 305-247-5727

Key Largo
   John Pennekamp Coral Reef State Park
   http://thefloridakeys.com/parks/pennekamp.htm
   Key Largo m.m. 102.5   305 451-1202

Key West
   Audubon House and Gardens **http://www.audubonhouse.com**
   205 Whitehead Street, Key West, 33040-6522   305-294-2116

   Bahia Honda State Park
   http://thefloridakeys.com/parks/ bahia.htm
   Bahia Honda Key m.m. 37   305-872-2353

   Dry Tortugas National Park **http://www.nps.gov/drto/**
   Fort Jefferson   305-442-7700

   Ernest Hemingway Museum
   907 Whitehead Street   305-294-1575

Nancy Forrester's Secret Garden
http://www.xnet.com/~graphics/secret/index.html
1 Free School Lane   305-294-0015

Sonny McCoy Indigenous Park
1801 White Street   305-292-8157

West Martello Gardens
Atlantic Boulevard by White St. Pier   305-294-3210

Lignumvitae Key]
Lignumvitae Key State Botanical Site
http://thefloridakeys.com/parks/lignum.htm
Lignumvitae Key m.m. 78.5   305 664-4815

Long Key
Long Key State Recreation Area
http://thefloridakeys.com/parks/long.htm
Long Key m.m. 67.5   305 664-4815

Melbourne
Florida Institute of Technology Botanical Gardens
150 W. University Boulevard, 32901-6982   407-768-8000

Miami Area
Barnacle State Historic Site
http://miami.info-access.com/barnacle.htm
3485 Main Hwy, Coconut Grove, 33133   305-448-9445

Fairchild Tropical Garden **http://www.ftg.org**
10901 Old Cutler Road, Miami, 33156-4233   305-667-1651

Garden of Our Lord
Saint James Evangelical Lutheran Church
110 Phoenetia Avenue, Miami, 33134-3312   305-443-0014

Gardens and Cloisters of the Monastery of Saint Bernard
16711 W. Dixie Hway, Miami, 33160-3714   305-945-1461

Japanese Teahouse and Garden
Watson Park (across MacArthur Causeway)   Miami

Kampong **http://www.ntbg.org**
4013 S. Douglas Road, Miami, 33133-6840   305-442-7169

Merrick House and Gardens
907 Coral Way, Coral Gables, 33134   305-460-5361

Miami Metrozoo
12400 SW 152nd Street, Miami, 33177   305-251-0400

Monkey Jungle
14805 SW 216th Street, Miami, 33170-2299   305-235-1611

Vizcaya Museum
http://www.artcom.com/museums/nv/sz/33129.htm
3251 S. Miami Avenue, Miami, 33129-2831   305-250-9133

Ochopee
Big Cypress National Preserve **http://www.nps.gov/bicy/**
52105 Tamiami East, Ochopee, 34141   941-695-4111

Palm Beach Area
Cluett Memorial Gardens
Bethesda by the Sea Church
141 S. County Road, Palm Beach, 33480-6107 561-655-4554

Mounts Botanical Gardens **http://www.mounts.org**
531 N. Military Trail, West Palm Beach, 33415-1395
561-233-1749

The Society of the Four Arts **http://pbol.com/4arts/main.html**
2 Four Arts Plaza, Palm Beach, 33480-4102   561-655-2776

Pompano Beach
Fern Forest Nature Center
http://www.co.broward.fl.us/pri01400.htm

201 Lyons Road South, Pompano Beach, 33068   954-970-0150

Societies and Associations

The American Hibiscus Society: **http://www.trop-hibiscus.com**
Florida Federation of Garden Clubs: **http://www.ffgc.org**
Audubon Society: **http://www.audubon.org**
Association for Tropical Lepidoptera Home Page: **http://www.troplep.org/atl.htm.**
The North American Butterfly Association: **http://www.naba.org**
National Wildlife Federation: **http://www.nwf.org**
Association of Florida Native Nurseries: **http://www.members.aol.com/afnn**
Florida Native Plant Society: **http://www.flmnh.ufl.edu/fnps/fnps.htm**

Other Related Environmental Sites

Animal and Plant Health Inspection Service: **http://www.aphis.usda.gov**
Pesticide Information (University of Florida, IFAS Pesticide Information Office): **http://fshn.ifas.ufl.edu/links.htm**
EPA: **http://www.epa.gov**
Florida Environments: **http://www.enviroworld.com**
Center for Aquatic and Invasive Plants (University of Florida, IFAS) **: http://aquat1.ifas.ufl.educ/**
South Florida Water Management District:
http://www.sfwmd.gov.

Add your own favorites: